ASSIMILATION PATTERNS OF IMMIGRANTS IN THE UNITED STATES:

A Case Study of Korean Immigrants in the Chicago Area

Won Moo Hurh
Hei Chu Kim
Kwange Chung Kim

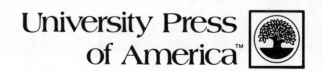
University Press of America™

Library of Congress Catalog Card Number: 78-59860

ASSIMILATION PATTERNS OF IMMIGRANTS IN THE UNITED STATES:

A CASE STUDY OF KOREAN IMMIGRANTS IN THE CHICAGO AREA

Won Moo Hurh
Hei Chu Kim
Kwang Chung Kim

ACKNOWLEDGMENTS

We wish to acknowledge our indebtedness to our interviewees
and interviewers for their time, effort, and cordial cooperation.
Our sincere thanks are due to the staff of Small Grant Section,
National Institute of Mental Health, especially of Dr. Stephanie
B. Stolz for her kind help rendered to us at the initial stage
of our research proposal. We wish to thank also the staff of
Research Office, Western Illinois University for their generous
assistance and Mrs. Susan Kennedy and Mrs. Sheila Morath for
typing the final copy of our manuscript. As Korean Americans
ourselves, we would like to express our special gratitude and
pleasure to the Department of Health, Education, and Welfare for
the grant (#R03 MH 27004) which enabled us to complete this
research in the bicentennial year of the United States. A con-
densed version of this study was presented at the National Con-
ference on "The New Immigration: Implications for American
Society and the International Community," Smithsonian Institu-
tion, Washington, D. C., November 15-17, 1976.

February 1978   Won M. Hurh
Western Illinois University   Hei C. Kim
Macomb, Illinois   Kwang C. Kim

ii

TABLE OF CONTENTS

LIST OF TABLES

LIST OF FIGURE

I. INTRODUCTION

The first wave of 7,226 Korean immigrants reached the
Hawaiian shores during the period of 1903-1905; however, the number of _bona fide_ immigrants[1] was relatively insignificant thereafter until 1958 (cf. Warren Kim, 1971; Hyung-Chan Kim, 1974)
when it increased more than two-fold from the previous year (from
648 in 1957 to 1,604 in 1958). The Korean government's restric-
tion on emigration (November 1905), the Japanese occupation of
Korea (1910-1945), the American immigration quota levied against
non-Europeans (1924-1965), and the Korean War (1950-1953) may
account for this phenomenon. For the following ten years (1958-
1968), the Korean immigration rate showed a steady growth rate
of two-fold, but then jumped to a phenomenal seven-fold rate
during the next five-year period, 1969-1974.[2] In 1974 alone,
28,028 Koreans emigrated to the United States, and the trend
may persist by virtue of the revised U.S. immigration legislation
(PL 89-236 of 1965) that has had a similar effect on other
Asian immigrants.

---

[1]Bona fide immigrants refer to those who entered the U.S.
with immigrant visas. Others include non-immigrants, such as
students, exchange visitors, diplomatic persons, political refu-
gees, illigal migrants, etc.

[2]Number of Korean immigrants to the U.S., 1964-1974 (Source:
U.S. Department of Justice, _Annual Reports_, Immigration and Naturalization Service):

1964	2,362	1967	2,956	1970	9,314	1973	22,930
1965	2,165	1968	3,811	1971	14,297	1974	28,028
1966	2,492	1969	6,045	1972	18,876		

If the 1970 Census report on Korean population (70,000)[1] were correct, there would have been 126,100 Korean residents in 1973, an increase of 80% in three years. And if the same trend continued for the following three years there would now be 182,000 or well over 200,000 Koreans residents in the United States in 1976, taking the other additive factors into consideration: such as natural increase and the changes in visa statuses of non-immigrants to that of permanent resident. As the recent H.E. & W. report predicts, there will be over a quarter of a million Korean residents in the United States by 1980 with the possibility of becoming the fourth largest Asian group in the country (U.S. Department of H.E. & W., 1974:32). Furthermore, some drastic changes in the socio-economic composition of recent immigrants over immigrants in previous years might be expected.

Although Korean immigrants seem to be more dispersed geographically than other Asian counterparts, the substantial majority of them are concentrated in metropolitan areas, such as Los Angeles, New York, Honolulu, and Chicago. In the metropolitan area of Chicago alone, some 25,000 Koreans establish their permanent homes today (The Hankuk Ilbo Miju News, 1975:1). In the last several years, they have been moving into the old Japanese neighborhood (North Clark Street), effecting a new type of natural

---

[1]The 1970 Census represents the first time that Koreans were enumerated as a separate ethnic group. "The total Census figures on Koreans vary from 69,510 to 70,598 (in both cases excluding the State of Alaska) due to the limited size of the sample" (U.S. Department of H.E. & W., 1974:132). See also Hyung-Chan Kim's figure of 68,216 (1974:36).

2

area and a new pattern of ecological succession. The similar
trends can be observed in the inner-cities of other metropolitan
areas (e.g., Olympic Boulevard in Los Angeles).

Until the early 1960's the geographic and social mobilities
of Korean residents in the United States (mostly in Hawaii and
on the West Coast) were relatively insignificant, compared to
those of other minorities (e.g., Japanese-Americans, Chinese-
Americans, or Filipino-Americans). However, the rapidly increasing
number of Korean immigrants and their geographic and social mobilities seem to alter the fabric of interethnic relations in the
major metropolitan areas.

The Korean immigrants share the common marginality with other
Asian ethnic groups; however, they seem to be subjected to a
severer sense of marginality. Unlike the other recent Asian immigrants from Hong Kong, the Philippines, India, and Pakistan, the
Korean immigrants are extremely handicapped by their unfamiliarity
with the Western culture in general and in the use of English
language in particular, largely because Korea has never had any
Anglo-American colonial experience. Moreover, they as an ethnic
group seem to be accorded   an extremely low social prestige by
the Americans in general, although the recent Korean immigrants
are the most highly educated among the Asian immigrants (U.S.
Department of H.E. & W., 1974: 25, 70, 105, 134). The empirical
studies of social distance repeatedly demonstrate that the
American people want even less association with the Koreans than
with other Asian groups (Bogardus, 1968). The problems of Korean

3

immigrants are compounded by the fact that they are the latest
arrivers among the Asian immigrants without a traditionally established foothold (e.g., "China Town" or "Little Tokyo").[1] In
addition to such objective marginality, the Korean immigrants also
suffer the subjective marginality which other first-generation
immigrants have suffered. As was mentioned earlier, approximately
two-thirds of Korean residents in the United States today came
from Korea after 1970. Cultural ambivalence, fear of social rejec-
tion, and identity crisis are the manifestation of the marginality.
Their problem represents a typical case of "Marginal Man."

Of special note with regard to the recent Korean immigrants
is their diversity. They include a large number of professionals
(e.g., physicians, nurses, engineers and the like), as well as a
significant number of Korean students in the United States, who,
upon the completion of their training, change their visa status
to immigrant status every year. Also joining the wave of immigration in increasing numbers is the group of semi-skilled and skilled
workers, who had been negligible as recent as the late 1960's.
Then there is the group of Korean wives of American servicemen
and their children.

Given the circumstances described above, one may wonder how
the Korean immigrants adjust themselves to the American way of life.

---

[1]Although some Korean ethnic enclaves are emerging, such as
"the Second Seoul" in Los Angeles and "Korea Town" in Chicago,
they are still in the formative stage (cf., Yoshihara, 1976;
The Joong-ang Daily News, February 6, 1976; Jade, December, 1975:
22-23).

4

More specifically, one might be curious about the differential patterns of cultural and social adjustment among the recent Korean immigrants as related to such variables as sex, age, marital status, education, occupation, income, and duration of stay in the United States, etc.

Unfortunately, very little research has been done of the Korean immigrants in the United States, although many studies have been done on the Korean War. A number of sociologists have recently made some valuable contributions by publishing their exploratory studies on Japanese and Chinese Americans in Prentice-Hall's Ethnic Groups in American Life Series (Kitano, 1976), Random House's Ethnic Groups in Comparative Perspective (Petersen, 1971; Lyman, 1974), and Wadsworth's Minorities in American Life (Hsu, 1971). On Korean Americans, however, no comprehensive study has been published to date.[1] When an entire volume of The Journal of Social Issues (1973, Vol. 29, No. 3) exclusively devoted to the study of Asian Americans under the title, "Asian Americans: A Success Story?," Koreans again were not included. In the editors' words: "Other groups such as the Filipinos and Koreans have not been studied as thoroughly; we regret that they thus can not be included in the analysis" (Kitano and Sue, 1973:3). The present

---

[1]Very recently Kim and Condon (1975) conducted extensive research on Asian Americans in Chicago in terms of social service needs but from social work and welfare perspectives. Cha's study (1975) on the Koreans in Los Angeles offers a valuable insight for re-examining Milton Gordon's assimilation typology, however, it suffers from an inadequate sample and the lack of intensive sociological analyses. Hyong-Chan Kim's study (1974) may be considered one of the most extensive studies on Korean immigrants but again is limited only to the demographic dimension.

study hopes to meet such a need in the American minority studies,
to promote interethnic understanding in the American society at
large, and to generate social policy implications for solving
ethnic community problems. Similar studies will be undertaken by
the present investigators for Korean immigrants in Los Angeles
and New York areas when further funding becomes available.

The main purpose of this study is, therefore, to describe and
analyze the differential patterns of cultural and social adjustment
among the Korean residents in the Chicago area. On the descriptive
level, it examines the general life changes and life styles of the
Korean immigrants in the Chicago area in terms of structural
variables (i.e., age, marital status, socioeconomic status, residence, religious affiliation, etc.) and survey the degree of cultural and social adjustment in terms of objective (behavioral) and
subjective (attitudinal) indices. On the analytical level, a
series of hypotheses are tested to examine relationships between
structural variables and the differential cultural and social
adjustment patterns.

6

II. DESIGN OF THE STUDY

A. Theoretical Framework and Hypotheses

Due to the paucity of previous studies and literature on the
Korean immigrants as noted earlier, the present study was meant to
be primarily exploratory in nature, based mainly on the general
theory of assimilation advanced by Milton Gordon (1964) and on the
recent studies on the relationship between structural variables
and acculturation rates by Alexander Weinstock (1963), Ronald J.
Silvers (1965), and Erich Rosenthal (1960). For a comparative
perspective, references are also made to other Oriental minority
studies, such as Kitano's Japanese-Americans: Evolution of a
Subculture (1969), Hsu's The Challenge of the American Dream:
The Chinese in the United States (1971), and Lyman's Chinese
Americans (1974).

The basic theoretical proposition for this study derived from
Gordon's distinction between "cultural assimilation" and "structural assimilation." According to Gordon, the former refers to
the change of cultural patterns to those of the host society and
the latter to the large-scale entrance into cliques, clubs and
institutuions of host society, on primary group level (1964:71).
Gordon argues that while acculturation (Gesellschaft type of intergroup relations) has taken place in America to a considerable
degree, structural assimilation (Gemeinschaft type of intergroup
relations) has not been extensive (cf. also Rosenthal, 1960).

7

This has been true for all ethnic minorities including the Jewish Americans, but more so for the non-white minorities (cf. Kitano, 1969). The persisting pattern of racial endogamy and social distance on primary group level attest to the fact (Goldstein and Goldscheider, 1968; Kitano, 1969; Simpson and Yinger, 1972).

Our first hypothesis is based on Gordon's general theory but more specifically on Weinstock's (1963) and Silver's (1965) propositions that the higher the occupational status, the greater the range of peripheral role elements there will be and that the greater the range of peripheral role elements, the greater the pressures and opportunities there will be for internalizing and displaying related social norms and beliefs of the host society. From this proposition we derived the following hypothesis:

> Hypothesis 1: Among Korean immigrants, those with high SES (socio-economic status) achieve a higher degree of cultural assimilation than those with low SES.

Gordon suggests that a high degree of acculturation does not necessarily lead to a high degree of social assimilation, while the reverse is true. For example, a highly acculturated Korean immigrant with a high SES (Hypothesis 1) may not necessarily achieve a high degree of social assimilation. Kitano's study of the Isseis (the first generation Japanese immigrants) indicates the similar phenomenon: regardless of their occupational mobility and concomitant acculturation they remain or "forced" to remain outside of the WASP (White Anglo-Saxon Protestant) Gemeinschaft.

8

This would mean, then, the socio-economic variables may have little or no direct effect upon the degree of social assimilation, although they may be significantly related to cultural assimilation. Thus, our second hypothesis is formulated as follows:

Hypothesis 2. Social assimilation is not related to socio-economic status among Korean immigrants.

Since Lenski's article on "status crystallization" (1954), Goffman (1957), Lenski (1964, 1966), Treiman (1966) and more recently Olsen and Tully (1972) have explored the sociological significance of status inconsistency. One of the most significant findings is that status inconsistency is strongly related to political and economic liberalism. A Korean immigrant doctor, for example, may rise on his professional and income ladder but still be subjected to social barriers over which he has no control. He may become highly acculturated gesellschaftlich but not a full-fledged member of the WASP Gemeinschaft.

"Hence, his only recourse - should he wish to escape his status inconsistency - will be to seek broad-scale social change through political action" (Olsen and Tully, 1972:562). The recourse to political action, however, largely depends on the size of minority group involved and the individual's perception of a political efficacy. When the status inconsistent individual is a member of a small minority group, he is more likely to feel powerless and any political action for him would become a remote possibility. In such a situation, his sense of relative deprivation and frustration would not likely be canalized into direct political action. Rather, it would most likely accentuate his own ethnic Gemeinschaft. Under such circumstances, his desire to become assimilated into host society would diminish in both dimensions: cultural and social assimilations. Senter (1945) noticed this tendency among the Spanish-Americans and Silvers (1965:72) confirmed it: "...the elites among the minority ethnic group, have slower acculturation rates than the stratum immediately below...."

The problem of status inconsistency among Korean immigrants has a unique dimension, that is, the inconsistency between pre-emigration SES in Korea and post-emigration SES in the United States. Due to the social and cultural handicaps described earlier, a significant number of Korean immigrants is subjected to underemployment. A college-educated government employee in Korea who immigrated to the United States and works as a factory hand is a case in point. He is subjected to "double status inconsistency," so to speak, since his present occupational status is not only discrepant with his occupation in Korea but also with his educational status. His range of peripheral role elements is extremely limited, hence his chances for social assimilation are extremely slim. While the Korean physician can retain his ethnic identity more or less by choice, the college-educated Korean factory hand is forced to remain a "Korean." Thus our third hypothesis is:

Hypothesis 3: Among Korean immigrants, status inconsistency affects the degree of both social and cultural assimilation.

It has been generally accepted that the longer the immigrant's sojourn in his host society, the higher will be the degree of his social and cultural assimilation. However, we maintain, with Tamar Becker (1968) who studied the attitudinal changes among foreign students in the United States, that there is a limit to the degree of social and cultural assimilation in spite of upward mobility and the consequent increased range of peripheral role elements. This contention is tantamount to asserting that there is no direct linear correlation between the length of sojourn and the degree of cultural and/or social assimilation (cf. Glazer, 1954). Although the process of assimilation may be progressive to a point, especially the initial period of adjustment and subsequent occupational advancement, we suspect that the process might not continue beyond a certain point, especially among professionals. As the immigrant moves up on the occupational ladder, he may increasingly experience his marginal status in his occupational milieu. The resultant sense of relative deprivation and frustration may further alienate him from the Gemeinschaft of his occupational colleagues, making him a victim of his own aspiration that could not be fulfilled. To mitigate this situation, the immigrant may seek his identity and reference group elsewhere. At this point his desire for Anglo-conformity may start to diminish. If this is true, then the relationship

11

between the length of sojourn and the degree of acculturation and social assimilation may be curvilinear rather than linear. From this theoretical argument our fourth hypothesis is derived:

> Hypothesis 4: There is no direct linear relationship between the length of sojourn in the United States and the degree of cultural and social assimilation among the Korean immigrant.

B. Method

Sampling and Interviewing

The data for the study were obtained from the Korean population in the Chicago metropolitan area,* which was estimated to be 15,000 in 1975. Originally, 500 were to be randomly selected as the sample, but the sample size had to be eventually reduced to 283 due to a number of unexpected difficulties encountered during the sampling and interviewing process.

Contrary to our expectations, no comprehensive and up-to-date directory of Korean immigrants in the area was available at either the Korean Consulate or at the Census Bureau. The Immigration and Naturalization Service in Chicago was approached without any result. Then, the Korean-language daily in Chicago, Hankuk Ilbo, was also approached in hope of obtaining its

---

*In consideration of feasibility and expediency for this study, the Chicago metropolitan area was operationally defined to include the inner city of Chicago and some 70 small suburban communities located within the 15-mile radius of the city of Chicago.

12

subscription list, but the efforts proved to be fruitless. A number of ethnic organizations were then approached for their membership directories. Most of these organizations, including the Korean Association of Chicago, Korean churches, alumni associations, Korean Ministers Association, Korean Nurses Association, and a golf club obliged with the request. In addition, the Chicago area telephone directories were used.

When overlapping memberships and those living outside the predefined radius were eliminated, a list of 3,397 was obtained. The random sampling technique was used to select 624 as the sample. The overdrawing of the sample was done in expectation of a refusal rate of at least 20% and some incorrect addresses.

Further difficulty was encountered in the process of interviewing. Of the carefully selected 624 individuals, 140, or 22%, were found to have wrong addresses, leaving no forwarding addresses for our interviewers to follow up. Some cases of incorrect addresses were expected at the outset, but the actual cases turned out to be significantly in excess of our expected level.

Of the remaining 484 individuals, 165, or 26% of the original sample, either could not be reached despite repeated attempts, or refused to be interviewed for one reason or another. The reasons for refusing interview may be divided into three general categories: (1) busy routine ("I just don't have such time to sit with you for an interview."; (2) apathy ("I am not interested in being interviewed"); and (3) suspicion ("Who is doing this survey?" or "Why is this survey being done?").

13

A total of 319 individuals was finally reached and interviewed. In cases where the respondents lived with their spouses,
males were interviewed when their identification numbers were
even and females when their numbers were odd, in order to insure
an even representation of males and females in the sample. Of
the completed questionnaires, 36 proved to be incomplete in terms
of certain specific information requested and hence were discarded.
Thus, 283 -- 169 males and 114 females -- constitute the sample
population, providing the basis of the present study.

In order to describe the problems encountered by the Koreans
and to establish relationships between their demographic characteristics and social and cultural assimilations, two questionnaires were developed to measure the degree of cultural and
social assimilations. The Cultural Assimilation Questionnaire
was comprised of 11 four or five-point items that were intended
to measure the degree to which respondents favor American cultural
traits. The Social Assimilation Questionnaire, consisting of
11 five-point items, was intended to measure the degree to which
respondents associate themselves with Americans on primary group
level. The questionnaire items were then translated into Korean
by the investigators themselves who are all native-born Koreans.

The translated version of the items were administered to 32
immigrants for pre-testing in order to refine wordings of the
items. On the basis of suggestions and comments given by the
respondents, a number of questions was reworded, added or eliminated. Out of the pre-test emerged the final version of ques-

14

tionnaires composed of 11 four or five-point items for cultural
assimilation and 11 five-point items for social assimilation.
(See Appendix)

A total of nine interviewers - five males and four females -
was selected from the Chicago metropolitan area on the basis of
their experiences in or familiarity with interviewing technique
as social science students or as insurance salesmen. Immediately
before the administration of the questionnaires began, the interviewers were brought to training sessions with the investigators
in order to (1) acquaint them with the objective of the study,
(2) to alert them to certain possible biases and errors, and (3)
to acquaint them with the certain techniques for developing rap-
port with their interviewees. These training sessions were pub-
licized in the Korean-language daily, Hankuk Ilbo, to inform the
Korean population in the area of the forthcoming survey.

Shortly after the training sessions, letters were sent to
respondents explaining in very general terms the nature of the
study and asking for their cooperation. Approximately ten days
were allowed to insure that the respondents received the letters
and still lived at given addresses. The interviewers then
visited their homes and either interviewed them there, if allowed,
or made appointments for interviews for later dates. At every
interview, the respondents were strongly assured that no one,
not even the investigators themselves, could identify certain
information with any particular respondents.

15

Included in the set of independent variables for this study
is inconsistency between the two major status dimensions of education and occupation.[1] Repondents were asked the number of
years of formal education they had completed and their present
occupation. The reponse to these questions were coded into six
categories for education and four categories for occupation: for
education, (1) some graduate school and more, (2) college, (3)
some college, (4) vocational school, (5) high school, and (6)
primary school or less; and for occupation, (1) professionals,
(2) white collar, (3) blue collar, and (4) others.

---

[1]Income was excluded from the analysis due to incomplete
and inaccurate information. Reasons for this exclusion will be
explained later (See page 57).

III. DESCRIPTIVE OVERVIEW

A. Demographic Characteristics

Age Distribution

The age distribution by sex for our sample is presented in
Table 1. On the whole, the respondents range in age from 20 to
74, with a median age of 36. Between the two sex groups, some
notable differences can be observed: (1) for the males the
median increases to 34 with a range from 19 to 74; and (2) for
the females the median decreases to 34 with a range from 21 to
65. More conspicuous is the 31-40 age category in both sex groups.
This is more pronounced among the males (62%) than among the
females (47%). Both sexes taken together, better than half of
the sample are in the age category 31 to 40.

Table 1. Respondents' Age by Sex

Age	Males		Females		Total	
	N	%	N	%	N	%
20 & under	2	1.1	-	-	2	0.1
21-31	24	14.2	39	34.2	63	22.3
31-40	105	62.0	54	37.3	159	56.2
41-50	30	18.1	14	12.3	44	15.5
51 & over	8	4.6	7	6.2	15	5.3
Total	169	100.0	114	100.0	283	100.0
	Mean:	37.25	Mean:	34.87	Mean:	36.06
	S.D.:	10.26	S.D.:	10.40	S.D.:	10.35

17

Specific Korean age distribution for the Chicago area cannot be obtained since this breakdown is not available in census
or any other sources. However, a recent study of Asian minority
groups in Chicago (Kim & Condon, 1975) reports the similar age
distribution of a sample of Korean immigrants to that of the present study -- 73% of their male and 42% of their female respondents were found to be in the age category of 31 to 40.

Marital Status

An overwhelmingly large proportion of the repondents (86.5%)
is married, as Table 2 shows. Although comparison of our finding
with the Korean population in the Chicago area in particular and
the United States in general is impossible at this time due to
the lack of data, the finding is consistent with that of Kim and
Condon; 88.2% of their respondents were married.

Table 2. Marital Status

Marital Status	N	%
Single	32	11.6
Married	240	86.5
Divorced	2	0.9
Other	3	1.0
Total	277	100.0

Missing cases: 6

Length of Residence in Chicago and U.S.

Almost 85% of the respondents have lived in Chicago for six years or less, with a mean of 4.2 years, as depicted in Table 3.

Table 3.   Length of Residence in Chicago and U.S.

Number of Years	Chicago N	%	U.S. N	%
1 - 2	87	31.1	77	27.5
3 - 4	89	31.8	83	29.5
5 - 6	61	21.8	57	20.3
7 - 8	24	8.6	28	9.9
9 & more	19	6.7	36	12.8
Total	280	100.0	281	100.0
	Mean:	4.18	Mean:	4.76
	S.D.:	2.51	S.D.:	3.11
	Missing cases: 3		Missing cases: 2	

Comparison of the length of residence in Chicago with that in the U.S. reveals very little, if any, differences in all categories except the last.   This seems to indicate that most of the respondents have settled in the Chicago area since their arrival in the United States with little geographical mobility.   Only among those in the 9 & more years category indicate some degree of geographical mobility.

Occupational Status

Table 4 shows the repondents' occupations held in Korea at the time of their emigration and those held currently in the

19

United States. More than 73% of the respondents held professional
and white-collar occupations and only 1.4% blue-collar occupations when they emigrated from Korea. The rest (25%) were either
unemployed or nonemployed. When the respondents' pre-immigration
occupations are compared with their current occupations in the
United States, a definite change in the distribution emerges.
While there is little change in the professional category (8.5%
to 7.6%) significant changes are observed in the white collar and
blue collar categories. Sixty-five percent of the respondents
held white-collar occupations at the time of their immigration,

Table 4. Last Occupation in Korea and Current Occupation in U.S.

Occupation*	Korea		U.S.	
	N	%	N	%
Professional	24	8.5	21	7.6
White Collar	184	65.0	101	36.5
Blue Collar	4	1.4	87	31.4
Other	71	25.1	68	24.5
Total	283	100.0	277	100.0

Missing cases: 6

*Occupational categories:
Professional includes physicians, professors, ministers,
engineers, and CPAs. White collar includes nurses, tea-
chers, pharmacist, clerical, reporters, proprietors, mana-
gers, salesmen, computer programmers and social workers.
Blue collar includes manual workers (skilled, semi-skilled
and unskilled). Other includes the unemployed and the
nonemployed (students, housewives, and retired persons).

20

but only 36.5% of them currently hold the same level of occupation, a change of 28.5%. This downward mobility of the white collar workers has inflated the percentage of blue collars workers from 1.4 to 31.4. These findings seem to indicate that while Korean immigrants with professional expertise are little affected by various cultural barriers in their occupational pursuit in the United States, those with less than professional training are seriously handicapped.

Although it is impossible at this time to compare these findings with the current occupational distribution of Korean immigrants in the United States in general and the Chicago area in particular, data on the occupational distribution of Korean immigrants at the time of arrival are available. The U.S. Immigration and Naturalization Service (1965-1973) reports that of all Korean immigrants reporting an occupation on their arrival between 1965 and 1973, 79% were professional and white collar workers (U.S. Dept. of H. E. & W., 1974:141). Kim and Condon also report a similar finding: more than 70% of their respondents in Chicago held professional and white collar occupations before immigration.

Educational Status

Data on the educational level achieved by the respondents in Korea and the United States are presented in Table 5.

21

Table 5. Education Received in Korea and U.S.

Education	Korea		U.S.	
	N	%	N	%
Some Graduate School & more	13	4.6	39	13.8
College	207	73.2	15	5.3
Some College	-	-	11	3.9
Vocational School	-	-	20	7.1
High School	57	20.1	-	-
Primary School	6	2.1	-	-
None	-	-	198	69.9
Total	283	100.0	283	100.0

The vast majority of the respondents (77.8%) have received four years of college education or more in Korea. Only 30% of the respondents received some amount of education in the U.S. Of these, nearly one half received their graduate and professional training while the other half is split into three levels - some college, college, and vocational school -- with the latter dominating the other two levels.

According to the U.S. Census Bureau, 36% of the Korean residents in the U.S. have a college education, compared to 11% in the U.S. as a whole. This percentage is, of course, six years old and based on the total Korean population including the earlier immigrants and their offspring whose educational levels are generally lower than those of the recent immigrants. With regard to the educational level of Korean immigrants in the

Chicago area, both our own and Kim and Condon's findings lead to
an estimate that about 75% of them have college education or more.
These recent findings appear to suggest that as the influx of
Korean immigrants continues, the overall educational level for
the Korean population in the United States tends to rise, exacer-
bating the perennial problem of underemployment currently pre-
valent among recent immigrants.

Type of Residence

As Table 6 shows, the majority of Korean immigrants in the
Chicago area (69.9%) rent apartments, while almost 18% own their
own homes. Kim and Condon's findings are supportive of these
findings in the distribution pattern, but not in absolute
percentages. One notable discrepancy between the two sets of
findings is the proportion of respondents owning their own homes
- 17.6% in our sample and 7.9% in their sample. The discrepancy
seems to be accounted for by the fact that Kim and Condon's
sample was drawn from the City of Chicago alone, whereas our
sample was drawn from the City of Chicago as well as from a
number of outlying suburban communities.

Table 6. Type of Residence

Type of Residence	N	%
Own Home	49	17.8
Rent Home	34	12.3
Apartment	195	69.9
Other	1	--
Total	279	100.2

Missing cases: 5

23

Church Affiliation

The church affiliation of the respondents in both pre-immigration and post-immigration periods is summarized in Table 7.
A predominantly large proportion of the respondents (65.7%) is
currently affiliated with Protestant churches of various denomi-
nations and sects. This percentage sharply contrasts with that
of the respondents affiliated with Protestant churches when they
were in Korea (45.6%) - an increase of 20%. Conversely, the
percentage of those with no church affiliation decreases from
47% in Korea to 31.2% in the United States. In view of the
fact that only about 10% of the total population of Korea are

Table 7. Church Affiliation in Korea and U.S.

Religion	Korea		U.S.	
	N	%	N	%
Protestant	129	45.6	186	65.7
Catholic	21	7.4	8	2.8
None	133	47.0	89	31.5
Total	283	100.0	283	100.0

Christians, one can see a significant overrepresentation of
Christians in our sample.

This increased interest in church participation among the
respondents seems to be indicative of their need to mitigate the
stresses and tensions resulting from their sense of socio-cultural
estrangement. Just as Protestant sects proliferate in urban

24

centers to serve the needs of estranged individuals, so do the
Korean community churches in the Chicago area, which number
more than 40 today, performing the mediator role between the
immigrants and the larger host society.

B. Social and Cultural Characteristics

Proficiency in English Language

In order to assess the magnitude of language problems among
the respondents, they were asked to self evaluate their own
proficiency in speaking, reading and writing English. Results
are summarized in Table 8 below. Among the three categories of
English usage, the most serious problem faced by the respondents
seems to be the limited ability of speaking. The majority of
them (59.3%) rate their ability to speak English as less than

Table 8. Self-Evaluation of Proficiency in English

English Proficiency	Speaking		Reading		Writing	
	N	%	N	%	N	%
Fluent	16	5.7	43	15.2	25	8.8
Good	99	35.0	118	41.7	101	35.7
Fair	112	39.6	96	33.9	117	41.3
Poor	50	17.7	21	7.4	34	12.1
Not at all	6	2.0	5	1.8	6	2.1
Total	283	100.0	283	100.0	283	100.0

adequate (the "Fair," "Poor," and "Not at all" categories), compared to 43.1% in their reading ability and 55.5% in their writing ability. Despite these variations, it is apparent that about half of the respondents experience language difficulty in the use of both spoken and written English.

Use of English at Home

Table 9 shows the extent to which the respondents use English at their homes. Only 12.7% of them report using English either always or frequently, while the vast majority use it either occasionally or not at all. Based on comments of some respondents, we can conjecture that even among those reporting constant or frequent use of English at their homes significant proportion uses it only in communicating with their children who were either born in this country or lost a good command of Korean language during their sojourn here.

Table 9. Use of English at Home

Frequency	N	%
Always	4	1.4
Frequently	32	11.3
Occasionally	143	50.5
Never	104	36.8
Total	283	100.0

Exposure to American Printed Media

About half of the respondents subscribe to at least one newspaper and/or magazine, as Table 10 shows. Those who do not
subscribe to any media report that they occasionally buy them at
newsstands or borrow them from friends. When they were asked
what sections of their newspapers they favored almost half of them
said they favored political, economic, and cultural sections,
while the rest was split into the other four categories, with
advertisement readership dominating, as can be seen from Table
11.

When the respondents are broken down by sex, differential
response patterns emerge. Significantly large proportions of
male respondents favor political and economic sections than
female counterparts. Only in cultural and advertisement sections
are larger proportions of female respondents represented than their
male counterparts, suggesting that the male respondents are ex-
posed to different aspects of American culture from females.

Table 10. Exposure to American Printed Mass Media

Number of Subscriptions	Newspaper		Magazine	
	N	%	N	%
3 or more	3	1.1	14	5.0
2	26	9.2	39	13.9
1	110	39.0	90	31.8
None	144	50.7	140	49.3
Total	283	100.0	283	100.0

Table 11. Favorite Newspaper Sections by Sex

Sections	Male N	Male %	Female N	Female %	Total N	Total %
Political	41	23.3	9	8.3	50	17.6
Economic	46	26.1	14	13.0	60	21.3
Cultural	34	19.3	36	33.3	70	24.8
Sports	25	14.1	5	4.6	30	10.5
Advertisement	26	15.7	33	30.6	59	20.9
Comic	1	0.5	10	9.2	11	3.9
Others	2	1.0	1	1.0	3	1.0
Total	175	100.0	108	100.0	283	100.0

Frequency of Using Western Food

In order to further assess the degree of cultural assimilation among the respondents, they were asked to report the frequency of using Western food. As shown in Table 12, the majority
of them use western food either always or frequently for breakfast
and lunch (58.3% and 54.4% respectively), but the percentage drastically decreases to 6.7% for dinner. Some comments made by the
respondents seem to indicate that the discrepancy is due to expediency (almost necessity) rather than preference. Western
breakfast, compared to traditional Korean breakfast, is consider-
ably simple to prepare, hence time saving. Since the majority of
the respondents have to eat their lunch at or near their work
places, it is more convenient to bring a sack lunch than to bring
the traditional Korean lunch which is usually composed of rice

28

and some side dishes. Even if some could afford to eat at a Korean restaurant, the long travel time involved usually rules out this possibility for many of them. One can infer from these findings that for the majority of the respondents the traditional Korean food is predominantly preferred over Western food, while Western food is utilized for convenience.

Table 12. Frequency of Using Western Food

Frequency	Breakfast		Lunch		Dinner	
	N	%	N	%	N	%
Always	105	37.1	109	38.5	8	2.8
Frequently	60	21.2	45	15.9	11	3.9
Occasionally	62	21.9	73	25.8	69	24.4
Never	56	19.8	56	19.8	195	68.9
Total	283	100.0	283	100.0	283	100.0

Organizational Membership

One of the widely recognized measures for social assimilation is organizational membership. To ascertain the degree of their social assimilation, the respondents were asked to name the organization(s) they belonged to, excluding professional and trade organizations. Results are provided in Table 13. Although a large proportion of them (65%) belongs to organizations of one sort or another, membership is largely limited to Korean ethnic organizations with Korean churches dominating (56.9%). Only a small minority (3.2%) belongs to American

29

churches which are the only non-Korean organizational type represented. These findings seem to present strong evidence that social relationships among the respondents are built around ethnic organizations, especially churches, within the well-defined boundaries of a Korean enclave.

Table 13. Organizational Membership

Organization	N	%
Korean Church	161	56.9
American Church	9	3.2
Others*	14	4.9
None	99	35.0
Total	283	100.0

*Alumni Associations, Korean Nurses Association, Korean Pharmacist Association, golf club, fishing club

Mere membership in organization(s) does not provide sufficient information on the degree of involvement in organizational activities. Further, since Korean churches have been established as the center of the Korean community, comparison of church attendance when in Korea with that in the United States would provide an insight into the multifarious roles played by Korean churches. To this end, the respondents were asked how often they attended church services when they were in Korea and currently in the United States. Results are provided in Table 14.

30

Table 14.   Church Attendance in Korea and U.S.

Frequency	In Korea		In U.S.	
	N	%	N	%
Every week	107	37.8	115	40.6
Twice a month	35	12.4	56	19.8
Once a month	13	4.6	13	4.6
4 to 5 times a year	18	6.4	17	6.0
Never	110	38.8	82	29.0
Total	283	100.0	283	100.0

As expected, the percentage of the respondents attending church services every week or twice a month increases from 50.2% in Korea to 60.4% in the United States. Conversely, the percentage of them not attending church services at all decreases from 38.8% in Korea to 29% in the United States. This means that more than 70% of the respondents are involved in Korean churches in varying degrees. Of those involved in Korean churches, 20% report being active in other church affairs such as teaching Sunday school classes, singing in church choirs, or serving on church committees.

The respondents were further asked an open-ended question to identify the satisfying aspects of involvement in church. The responses to the questions were categorized into four general categories, as shown in Table 15.

31

Table 15. The Satisfying Aspects of Involvement in Churches

Type of Satisfaction*	N	%
Social	38	34.0
Psychological	31	27.7
Personality	8	7.1
Religious	35	31.2
Total	112	100.0

Missing cases: 89

*Social - include "friendship, "fellowship," "social gathering,"
        "relief of social isolation."
 Psychological - includes "psychological comfort," "security,"
        "comfort."
 Personality - includes "personality growth," "personality
        development."
 Religious - includes "worship of God," "expression of faith,"
        "experience of God's grace."

Of those who answered the question, the majority (68.8%)
identify non-religious satisfaction as the benefit they derive
from their involvement in church; only a small minority (31.2%)
identifies religious satisfaction as such. Thus, these findings
seem to support our suspicion that Korean churches play an important role of accommodating Korean immigrants to their host society,
in addition to meeting their religious needs.

Presence of Close Friends

        Closely related to organizational participation as a measure
of social assimilation is the presence of close friends outside
of an ethnic group. For a comparative purpose, the respondents

32

were asked to report the number of both American and Korean friends whom they consider to be close to them. It can be seen from Table 16 that more than half do no have any American friend, while only 18.3% have no Korean friend. The differential clearly indicates that a considerable social distance exists between the immigrants and the "majority" members of their host society.

Table 16. Presence of Close Friends

Number of Friends	American		Korean	
	N	%	N	%
4 or more	16	5.7	34	12.1
3	16	5.7	40	14.1
2	44	15.5	97	34.3
1	52	18.4	60	21.2
None	155	54.7	52	18.3
Total	283	100.0	283	100.0

In order to further assess the degree of social assimilation of the immigrants, information was obtained on the frequency of invitations (except business-related ones) extended by Americans to the immigrants and those extended by the respondents to Americans during the past year. Results are summarized in Table 17.

Comparison of the frequency of invitations extended by Americans to the immigrants with that of invitations extended by the immigrants to Americans reveals different patterns. While

33

slightly more than one third of the immigrants had never been invited by Americans, almost half had never invited Americans, indicating that more immigrants had been invited by Americans than vice versa.

Table 17. Frequency of Invitations Extended by Americans to the Immigrants and Those Extended by the Immigrants to Americans

Frequency in Past One Year	By Americans		By Immigrants	
	N	%	N	%
10 or more	10	3.6	11	3.9
7 - 9	11	3.8	7	2.5
5 - 6	28	9.8	20	7.1
3 - 4	40	14.0	31	10.9
Twice	48	17.0	39	13.8
Once	40	14.0	40	14.1
Never	106	37.8	135	47.7
Total	283	100.0	283	100.0
	Mean: 2.3		Mean: 1.8	
	S.D.: 3.4		S.D.: 2.7	

C. Attitudinal Patterns

In the previous section, attempts were made to assess the degree of social and cultural adjustment among the immigrants by inquiring into various behavioral patterns. Focus will be shifted in this section to attitudinal pattern in order to augment behavioral patterns reported at length in the previous section. Data were obtained through a series of questions designed to

34

elicit all three components of the respondents' attitudes -
cognitive, affective and conative - bearing upon social and
cultural adjustment.

Attitude Toward Some Korean Customs

Social and cultural adjustment implies abandoning some old
ways and adopting some new ones. In Table 18, responses to the
question, "Do you think some of our customs should no longer be
practiced because they delay acceptance of Koreans into American
society," are summarized.

Table 18. Attitude Toward Discarding Some Korean Customs

Attitude	N	%
Strongly agree	34	12.1
Moderately agree	130	46.4
Undecided	57	20.0
Moderately disagree	39	13.5
Strongly disagree	23	7.9
Total	283	100.0

The majority of the respondents (58.5%) agree either strongly or
moderately that some customs should be abandoned; only a little
more than one fifth disagree that they should.

Those who thought some customs should be abandoned were further asked to identify specific customs that they thought should

35

be abandoned. Heading the list of such customs is the traditional extended family system with its concomitants (the burden of familial obligations, traditional marital roles, authoritarian treatment of children and male dominance), followed by traditional rituals (ancestor worship, expensive wedding and other traditional ceremonies), cumbersome Korean cookery, and tardiness in order of frequency.

As an extension to eliciting the respondents' attitudes toward some specific aspects of Korean culture, a general and positive question was asked: "Do you think Korean language, history, morals, and customs should be taught to your children?" Table 19 shows that the vast majority of the respondents (95.1%) think they should be taught to their children. The fact that Korean culture is so important, as implied in these findings, for most of the immigrants seems to suggest their tenacity to preserve their ethnic identity and their desire to perpetuate it through generations.

Table 19. Attitude Toward Instructing Korean Language, History, Morals, and Customs to Children

Attitude	N	%
Strongly Agree	181	64.0
Moderately Agree	88	31.1
Undecided	9	3.2
Moderately disagree	-	-
Strongly disagree	5	1.7
Total	283	100.0

36

Attitude Toward Residing in Predominantly American Neighborhood

In the absence of exclusively Korean neighborhoods in the Chicago area, there is hardly any alternative to residing in predominantly American neighborhoods for the Korean immigrants. However, it would be helpful in understanding adjustment patterns of the immigrants if we knew something about how they feel about living with Americans as their neighbors. For this reason, the respondents were asked the question: "Would you feel more comfortable in predominantly American neighborhoods than Korean?" As Table 20 shows, the majority of them (58.6%) feel that they would be either uncomfortable or are not sure.

Table 20. Attitude Toward Residing in All-American Neighborhood

Attitude	N	%
Definitely yes	33	11.7
Probably yes	84	29.7
Undecided	69	24.4
Definitely no	73	25.8
Probably no	24	8.4
Total	283	100.0

Attitude Toward Making Friends With Americans

Closely related to the attitude toward residing in predominantly American neighborhoods is the attitude toward befriending Americans; a person with an attitude on the former would likely

37

have a positive attitude on the latter as well. When the respondents were asked the question, "Do you think Americans are easier to get along with than Koreans," 67% of them responded that they did not think so or were not sure. One may note in Table 21 that this response pattern is similar to that on the attitude toward residing in predominantly American neighborhoods.

Table 21. Attitude Toward Befriending Americans

Attitude	N	%
Definitely yes	22	7.8
Probably yes	72	25.2
Undecided	51	18.1
Probably no	74	25.9
Definitely no	65	23.0
Total	283	100.0

Attitude Toward Korean Children Playing With American Children

Would a similar attitude toward making friends with adult Americans reflect the attitude toward Korean children associating with American children? To answer this question, the respondents were asked, "Would you say it is better for your children to play with American children than with Korean children?" Evidence provided in Table 22 indicates that although the majority of the respondents are generally reserved or negative about befriending Americans, the overwhelming majority (74.6%) said that

38

it would be better for their children to associate with American children. The discrepancy might be suggestive of the respondents' differential expectations of themselves and their children with regard to their adjustment in the adopted society; the respondents seem to have stronger desire and hope for thier children to be assimilated into American society than for themselves.

Table 22. Attitude Toward Korean Children Playing
with American Children

Attitude	N	%
Definitely yes	63	22.2
Probably yes	147	52.4
Undecided	37	12.8
Probably no	24	8.4
Definitely no	12	4.2
Total	283	100.0

Attitude Toward Interracial Marriage With Americans

Interracial marriage signifies the least social distance between the two persons involved, as the Bogardus Social Distance Scale implies. In order to obtain information on how they felt about interracial marriage with Americans, the respondents were asked: "What do you think of interracial marriage between Koreans and Americans." Table 23 presents a summary of responses. Almost two-thirds of the respondents reported that they either disapprove or are not sure of it.

39

The respondents were further asked to give their reasons for either approving or disapproving of interracial marriage. Of those approving of it, well over two thirds of them identified love as the crucial factor in marriage, interracial or otherwise ("As long as two persons love and understand each other, nothing is wrong about interracial marriage."), while the rest pointed to the basic human nature according to which "all human beings are essentially the same." Among those disapproving, the most frequently expressed reason for disapproving of it is that "differences in race, custom, language and life-style are likely to lead to marital conflict and disorganization," followed by such reasons as "I don't want to have mixed-blood children," "I want to maintain racial and ethnic purity," and "Korean wife is better or more subservient."

Table 23. Attitude Toward Interracial Marriage
with Americans

Attitude	N	%
Strongly approve	13	4.7
Moderately approve	86	30.5
Undecided	41	14.3
Moderately disapprove	57	20.0
Strongly disapprove	86	30.5
Total	283	100.0

40

Desire to Retire in Korea

It can be logically argued that an immigrant who makes his adopted society his permanent home even after his retirement would be the one better adjusted to his host society than a person who returns to his country of origin upon retirement. Since the present study is concerned with the Korean immigrants who are currently residing in the United States, the respondents were asked whether they would return to Korea after their retirement. In Table 24 one can see that a large proportion of them (65.8%) have a desire of varying degrees to spend their retirement years in Korea; only 17.8% express their desire to remain in this country.

Table 24. Desire to Retire in Korea

Attitude	N	%
Definitely yes	109	38.4
Probably yes	78	27.4
Undecided	46	16.4
Probably no	32	11.4
Definitely no	18	6.4
Total	283	100.0

When asked for their reason for wanting to retire in Korea, the predominant reason given were the expected problems of adjustment and the emotional, social and political attachment to Korea ("I want to bury my bones in Korea," "I want to be with my

41

relatives and friends for the rest of my life," "I want to help Korea with what I have learned in this country"). Among those who expressed their desire to remain in this country, the vast majority pointed out their family network as their reason ("All my children and other family members will be living in this country."). only a small proportion (17%) cites the "satisfactory life in America" as their reason.

Perceived Opportunity in the United States

Based on the assumption that the immigrants's perceived opportunity in the United States is likely to be concomitant with their social and cultural adjustment, the respondents were asked if they thought there were opportunities for them in the United States, and if they did, in what areas. Because the question calls for more than a simple, spontaneous answer, 88 respondents did not answer it. Responses to the open-ended question are categorized and summarized in Table 25.

Nearly half of them (45.7%) see almost an unlimited opportunity in the United States, but they see such an opportunity restricted to professional, technical, and business fields and available only for those with special qualities including proficiency in English and American academic degrees among others. Slightly more than half of the respondents see some, little or no opportunity.

Table 25. Perceived Opportunity in the United States

Perceived Opportunity in the United States	N	%
Almost unlimited under qualified conditions*	10	5.1
Almost unlimited in technical & professional fields	41	21.0
Almost unlimited in business field only	38	19.6
Some, but limited	82	42.0
Little or no opportunity	24	12.3
Total	195	100.0

*This category includes "no language," "academic degrees from American universities," "extroverted personality" and "employment of both husband and wife."

Attitude Toward Anglicizing Korean Names

Would the Anglicization of Korean names among the immigrants have any bearing upon their adjustment in their host society? Answer to this question was sought by asking them how they felt about changing Korean names to American ones. Table 26 shows that about two thirds of the respondents approve of such a practice, while only one third disapprove.

When asked for their reasons for approving of such a practice almost every one of those who approve gave practical reasons ("It would be easier or more convenient for Americans to pronounce or remember," "It would be proper and convenient to have American names at workplaces," and "It would be proper to have an American name when I am naturalized.") Those disapproving of it are divided almost equally into two groups; one group gave

43

their alien status as the reason ("because I am not an American")
and the other cited their desire to preserve Korean identity as
the reason ("My name has been given by my parents," and "My name
signifies my Korean identity.")

Table 26. Attitude Toward Anglicizing Korean Names

Attitude	N	%
Strongly approve	38	13.4
Moderately approve	156	55.2
Undecided	4	1.4
Moderately disapprove	44	15.5
Strongly disapprove	41	14.5
Total	283	100.0

Perceived Attitude of Americans Toward the Respondents

One of the significant factors expediting or inhibiting the
immigrants' adjustment to his adopted society would be the way in
which he perceives his host's attitude toward him. Data were
collected by asking the respondents "Do you feel most Americans
accept you as their equal?" and are summarized in Table 27.

In contrast to empirical findings on social distance (Bogardus, 1968) where the reported rank for Koreans has consistently
been near the bottom of the scale, the majority of the respondents
(52.4%) feel that most Americans accept them as their equal, even
though most of them do not feel so definite about their answers;

44

only 30% of the whole sample feel that they are not accepted equally by Americans.

Table 27. Perceived Attitude of Americans Toward the Respondent

Perceived Attitude of Americans	N	%
Definitely yes	28	10.0
Probably yes	120	42.4
Undecided	50	17.5
Probably no	68	24.2
Definitely no	17	5.9
Total	283	100.0

Perceived Equity in Pay

Quite apart from the respondents' perception of general attitude (social acceptance) of Americans toward them, it would be useful to gain some insight into how they think about their own monetary remuneration as compared to their fellow workers. To this end, the respondents were asked the question, "Do you think your pay is comparable to that of your American fellow workers?" Their responses are summarized and presented in Table 28.

Consistent with their response pattern on Americans' attitude, the majority of the respondents (70.3%) think that they are not discriminated against in terms of monetary remuneration for their work, while a small proportion of them (13.9%) think they are.

45

Table 28. Perceived Equity in Pay

Perceived Equity in Pay	N	%
Definitely yes	65	31.1
Probably yes	82	39.2
Don't know	31	14.8
Probably not	29	13.8
Definitely not	2	0.1
Total	209*	100.0

* Only those employed at the time of interview. Those unemployed or non-employed, and six missing cases are not included in the total.

Perceived Status Inconsistency

In addition to assessing the variations in their perceived equity in pay among the respondents, attempts were made to obtain information on how they perceive their status in terms of inconsistent status components. For the purpose of this study, three status components were used; income, education and occupation. The respondents were first asked "Do you think your present income is commensurate with your education?" As can be seen from Table 29, there is no significant difference between those who perceive little or no inconsistency and those who do, even though the proportion of the former is a little larger than that of the latter (46.8% and 41.2%, respectively).

The respondents were also asked, "Do you think your occupation is commensurate with your education?" Their responses,

46

summarized in Table 30, indicate that here again the respondents' perception of status inconsistency between occupation and education is mixed. The response pattern is very similar to that on the inconsistency between income and occupation, with 48.8% perceiving little or no inconsistency and 45.5% perceiving it to varying degrees.

Given the fact that most of the respondents are underemployed, it is puzzling to find such a large proportion perceive little or no inconsistency in their status. One plausible explanation seems to be that the respondents, being newcomers in their adopted society, are not able to grasp the reality that belies them; the relatively high standard of living they enjoy in the United States tends to prevent any sense of relative deprivation from entering their consciousness in the early years of their immigrant life.

Table 29. Perceived Status Inconsistency
between Income and Education

Perceived Status Inconsistency	Between Income & Education	
	N	%
Definitely yes	35	16.7
Probably yes	63	30.1
Don't know	25	12.0
Probably no	51	24.5
Definitely no	35	16.7
Total	209	100.0

47

Table 30. Perceived Status Inconsistency
between Occupation and Education

Perceived Status Inconsistency	Between Occupation & Education	
	N	%
Definitely yes	51	24.4
Probably yes	51	24.4
Don't know	12	5.7
Probably no	42	20.1
Definitely no	53	25.4
Total	209	100.0

D. Problem Areas in Adjustment

The previous section, dealing with demographic, socio-cultural
characteristics, and attitudinal patterns, obviously suggest a
number of problem areas for the respondents either implicitly or
explicitly. The problems indirectly suggested by the data not-
withstanding, the question still remains as to what areas in the
immigrants' life they perceive as problematic. On the assumption
that whatever the respondents report as problem areas should
affect their adjustment in their adopted society, they were asked,
"What is the most important problem or difficulty you are experi-
encing in the course of your immigrant life?" Fifty-nine respondents either refused to answer the question or said they did not
have any problem. Responses of the rest of the respondents are
summarized in Table 31.

48

Table 31. The Most Important Problem or Difficulty
           Experienced by Respondents in Their Adjustment

Problem Areas	N	%
Language	106	47.3
Busy Routine	30	13.4
Concerns for Children	27	12.1
Social Isolation	19	8.5
Job-Related Problems	19	8.5
Inadequate Income	14	6.2
Racial Discrimination	9	4.0
Total	224	100.0

The vast majority of the respondents (79%) do experience at
least one problem of some types which they consider important.
As the table shows, the most frequently cited problem is that of
language - almost half of them (47.3%) report it as the most
important problem. Unlike the Filipino immigrant and other Asian
immigrants (e.g., Indians) who have had Anglo-American colonial
experiences, the Korean immigrant has never been accustomed to
the use of English. English, to be sure, is taught in high
schools and colleges in Korea, but its practical use is extremely
limited because of the emphasis on written English. As a result,
even a college graduate is frequently not competent in engaging in
simple conversations. It is no wonder then that such a large
proportion, though highly educated, experiences language
problems.

49

Immediately following the problem of language in the list of problem areas is the problem of busy routine which characterizes the urban life in industrialized society. Some 13% express that their busy routine - holding two jobs or going to school while working full time - put stress on their family and personal lives and often leads to despair due to mental and physical exhaustion.

Next to the problem of busy routine in order of frequency is concerns for children. Slightly more than 12% of the respondents identify their concerns for children's welfare and future as the most important problem. Specific concerns expressed by them include (1) children's general and learning experiences at school, (2) their adaptation to the American way of life, (3) their educational opportunity, (4) their future (expected) experience of racial discrimination, (5) generation gap between parents and children in the future, and (6) parent's inability to guide their children properly because of their lack of understanding of the American way of life.

The rest, or 27%, of the respondents are almost evenly distributed in four categories. One noteworthy finding is the extremely small proportion of them (6.2%) citing the problem of inadequate income as the most important problem. This finding is consistent with the data on status inconsistency discussed in the previous section, where it was found that despite prevailing underemployment among the respondents, most of them do not perceive any inconsistency among their status components. Consequently, most of them do not feel deprived and regard their income generally adequate.

IV. ANALYSIS OF DATA: HYPOTHESES TESTING

A. Construction of Variable Index

As described earlier, the Cultural Assimilation Questionnaire
consisted of 11 items and the Social Assimilation Questionnaire,
also 11 items. Since it was impractical to test each of them
against the hypotheses of this research, an attempt was made to
reduce the items to a limited number of factors by factor analysis
and with consideration of some conceptual and substantive issues
related to these items.

Cultural Assimilation Index

Through factor analysis, four factors were identified in the
Cultural Assimilation Questionnaire for the male respondents and
five for the females. The last factor from both male and female
respondents were eliminated from the subsequent analysis, since
they were found to be relatively insignificant. The remaining
factors are presented in Table 32.

In the first factor, three items revealed high factor-
loading for both male and female respondents. These items measure
their ability to speak, write and read English. Hereafter, the
first factor, composed of three items, will be referred to as
English Proficiency.

In the second factor, two items revealed high factor-loading
for both male and female respondents. The two items measure the

51

Table 32. Factor Analysis of Cultural Assimilation Items

Cultural Assimilation Items	Factor 1		Factor 2		Factor 3		Factor 4	
	M	F	M	F	M	F	M	F
Speaking English	.69	.75	.26	-.05	.35	.42		.08
Reading English	.86	.76	.11	.11	.16	.24		.02
Writing English	.79	.88	.01	.04	.28	.03		-.02
Subscription to Newspaper	.32	.28	.07	.17	.59	.61		-.08
Subscription to Magazine	.11	-.12	.04	.26	.48	.14		-.12
Use of English at Home	.23	.12	.22	.04	.37	.37		.15
Anglicization of Name	.15	.14	-.02	.08	.24	.11		.54
Western food for Brkfast.	.21	.17	.58	.70	.03	.01		.23
Western food for Lunch	-.01	.08	.74	.63	.08	.11		.23
Western food for Dinner	.05	.06	.38	.01	.19	.14		.05
Discarding Korean Custom	-.02	-.18	.07	.12	-.01	-.05		.48

M: Male respondents
F: Female respondents

frequency of using Western food for breakfast and lunch. This
factor, however, will not be used in the test of the hypotheses.
It was suspected that one of the two items carried two meanings.
When the respondents state that they do not use Western food at
all for breakfast, it could mean that they do not eat breakfast
at all. Their response could mean on the other hand, that they
always eat Korean food for breakfast. The second item (the
frequency of using Western food for lunch) again did not appear
to be a good instrument in measuring the degree of cultural assimilation, because most of the employed respondents would have
to eat lunch away from their homes.

In the third factor, four items revealed high or moderately
high factor-loading for the male respondents, and only three for
the female respondents. The first item measures English speaking
ability and is thus repeated from the first factor. The second
item concerns the number of American newspapers to which they
subscribe. The third item measures the frequency with which
respondents use English at home. The fourth item, which was
identified only among the male respondents, deals with the number
of American magazines to which they subscribe. These four items
suggest that the third factor concerns primarily the degree to
which respondents use English in conversation and in reading
American newspapers and magazines. Hereafter, this factor,
composed of the four items, will be referred to as Use of English.

The fourth factor contained two factor-loaded items only for
the female respondents. One item measures the degree of the

respondents' willingness to anglicize their first names. The
next item concerns the respondents' attitude toward discarding
those aspects of Korean customs which might cause them problems
in American life. This factor, which combines the two items,
will be hereafter referred to as Willingness to Discard Native
Customs. For the sake of consistency in the use of measurement
instruments for both male and female respondents, it will be
used for the male respondents as well.

Three factors - English Proficiency, Use of English, and
Willingness to Discard Native Customs - will thus be used as indices of cultural assimilation for testing the hypotheses. Each
of the selected items consisted of either four or five categories
in ordinal scale. Weight ranged from one to four or five was
assigned to the categories according to the magnitude of cultural
assimilation they represented.

Scores arrived at by this method range from three to fifteen
for English proficiency, from four to seventeen for the use of
English, and from two to ten for the willingness to discard
native customs.

Social Assimilation Indices

Out of the 11 items of social assimilation, only nine* were
usable for factor analysis. They consisted of two types of
items; the behavioral and attitudinal aspects of social assimilation.
(See Table 33)

---

*Two items were open-ended questions.

54

Table 33. Common Factor of Social Assimilation Identified Among both Male and Female Respondents

Social Assimilation Items	Common Factor	
	Male	Female
Preferred Neighborhood	.14	-.03
Making Friends with Americans	.45	.17
* Close American Friends	.44	.69
* Equal Treatment	.51	.53
Preferred Children's Playmates	-.10	-.01
Interracial Marriage	.14	.13
Plan to Retire in Korea	.07	.32
* Invitation by Americans	.77	.84
* Invitation by Immigrants	.75	.69

*Behavioral aspects of social assimilation.

All four items of the first type were clustered around the same factor. This observation is true for both male and female respondents. One of the items measures the frequency with which respondents were invited by Americans during the past year for social association. This item will hereafter be referred to as Invitation by Americans. Another item measures the frequency with which the respondents invited Americans to their homes for social association during the same year. This item will hereafter be referred to as Invitation by Immigrants. The above two items constitute interval scales and will be used as separate indices of social assimilation.

The remaining two items were combined to construct another index of social assimilation. One of these items concerns the number of American friends with whom the respondents feel they can confide, while the other measures the perceived degree of equal treatment of them by Americans. Hereafter this index will be referred to as Perceived Degree of Equal Treatment, whose score ranges from two to ten.

All other items of social assimilation do not reflect their behavior, which in the strict sense, do not test social assimilation as defined by Milton Gordon. They will therefore not be used in testing the hypotheses.

B. The Result of Hypotheses Testing

Three indices of cultural assimilation (CA indices) and

three indices of social assimilation (SA indices) have been constructed for testing the four hypotheses. Pearsonian correlation
coefficients between CA and SA indices were calculated in order
to examine the degree of their relationship. (See Table 34).

For the male respondents, all the CA indices show significant
correlations with all the SA indices at least at the .01 level.
The correlations are also generally significant when they are
controlled for by the length of sojourn in the United States.
The similar pattern is found for the female respondents except
one CA index (Willingness to Discard Native Customs).

> Hypothesis 1: Among Korean immigrants, those with
> high SES (socio-economic status) achieves a higher
> degree of cultural assimilation than those with low
> SES.

Due possibly to the respondents' misunderstanding of the
question on their annual incomes, inadequate data were collected:
some reported their own personal income and others the combined
income of their family members. For this reason, income as a
measure of SES is dropped. This left two measures of SES for
this research: education and occupation. Due to the paucity
of research on Korean immigrants, however, it is extremely
risky to construct a single index of SES based on these two
factors. Therefore, education and occupation will be used
separately in testing the three hypotheses (1, 2, and 3) that
deal with SES.

57

Table 34. Correlation Coefficients between SA and CA Indices and Partial Correlation Coefficients with the Length of Sojourn in the U.S. Controlled for.

CA Indices / SA Indices		English Proficiency				Use of English				Discarding Native Customs			
		male		female		male		female		male		female	
		A	B	A	B	A	B	A	B	A	B	A	B
Frequency of Invitation by Americans	r	.27	.11	.32	.28	.38	.22	.50	.41	.24	.23	.10	.05
	sig.	.001	.06	.001	.001	.001	.002	.001	.001	.001	.001	.13	.27
Frequency of Invitation by Immigrants	r	.26	.09	.33	.29	.41	.23	.50	.43	.17	.20	.06	.03
	sig.	.001	.11	.001	.001	.001	.001	.001	.001	.01	.004	.23	.36
Equal Treatment	r	.38	.26	.36	.31	.45	.31	.43	.30	.29	.16	.07	.02
	sig.	.001	.001	.001	.001	.001	.001	.001	.001	.001	.01	.20	.37

N(A): M = 169   F = 114
N(B): M = 165   F = 110

A: Correlation coefficient between the CA and SA indices.
B: Partial correlation coefficient with the length of sojourn in the U.S. controlled for.

The respondents were classified into three categories according to level of education. The first category consisted of those with bachelor's degrees from or some graduate work at American college or universities. In the second category were those respondents with bachelor's degrees from Korean institutions, but did not belong to the first category. The third category includes those respondents without any bachelor's degrees.

The respondents were also classified into three occupational categories: professionals, non-professional white collar workers and blue collar workers. Since there are no professionals among the female respondents, only two occupational categories were used for the women.

The three occupational categories were placed in rank order according to the level of occupational prestige found in America and many other societies (cf. Hodge, Treiman, & Rossi, 1966:309-321). Professionals are thus ranked highest and blue collar workers lowest.

It is possible to place the three educational categories in rank order, since most of the American-educated respondents (first category) had already obtained Korean bachelor's degrees before they began their American educational careers. It is, therefore, possible to rank the first category of respondents highest on the basis of the level of education, and the third category lowest.

Such classification inevitably exclude certain types of respondents from the test of Hypotheses 1 and 2. Specifically,

59

those who were not employed or those who failed to report their occupation or level of education in Korea were excluded. As a result, the testing of these hypotheses is based upon 119 male and 68 female respondents.

As expected, the level of education is found to be highly correlated with the level of occupational prestige. Furthermore, the level of education and that of occupational prestige are highly related to the length of residence in the U.S. Generally, the higher the level of educational or occupational prestige one has achieved, the longer he has resided in the U.S. (see Table 35). This suggests the need to use the time factor as a control variable for testing Hypotheses 1 and 2.

Table 35. Distribution of Means of Length of Residence by Sex, and Educational and Occupational Categories

| | | Male (N=119) | | Female (N=68) | |
		Mean	S.D.	Mean	S.D.
Level of Education	Higher Education in U.S.	7.63	3.18	6.44	1.74
	Higher Education in Korea	3.56	1.80	4.80	2.93
	No College Degree	3.58	2.74	4.81	4.12
Level of Occupation	Professional	7.00	4.12		
	Other White Collar	5.16	2.51	5.46	2.86
	Blue Collar	3.10	1.74	4.25	3.26

60

If hypothesis 1 is true, then those respondents with a high level of education or occupational prestige will show high CA scores. Table 36 shows the distribution of the male respondents in the three categories of education and occupational prestige, their CA mean scores (A) and an adjusted CA mean scores (B), and Table 37, three F values and levels of significance associated with them. The adjusted score refers to the mean score after the length of residence is controlled through multiple classification analysis. The first F values test the significance of differences in the CA mean scores by one-way analysis of variance. The second F values test the significance of difference in the CA mean scores by an analysis of covariance (the length of sojourn controlled for). The third F values test the significance level for the interaction effect resulting from the analysis of covariance.

Table 36 shows that there is a positive relationship between the level of education and the CA mean scores for the male respondents. The relationship remains the same after it is controlled for by the length of sojourn. When the mean scores are subjected to one-way analysis of variance, the differences in the mean scores for two CA indices (English Proficiency and the Use of English) is found to be significant (see Table 37). Further, the analysis of covariance shows no changes in the above analysis, revealing no interaction effect.

In terms of occupational prestige the test of significance of differences shows similar results. These analyses bear out our prediction that the SES indices are positively related to the

Table 36. Distribution of the CA Mean Scores by Education and Occupational Prestige (Male)

		English Proficiency		Use of English		Discarding Native Customs	
		A	B	A	B	A	B
Level of Education	Higher Education in U.S.	12.00	11.13	13.43	12.32	7.16	6.73
	Higher Education in Korea	10.38	10.68	11.71	12.02	6.56	6.61
	No College Degree	8.53	8.83	10.47	10.77	6.11	6.26
Level of Occupational Prestige	Professional	12.45	11.87	13.50	12.80	7.20	6.89
	Other White Collar	10.78	10.64	12.25	12.08	6.75	6.67
	Blue Collar	9.52	9.90	11.10	11.53	6.20	6.39

A: CA mean scores without the length of sojourn controlled.
B: CA mean scores with the length of sojourn controlled.

Table 37. F Values and Significance Levels for CA Indices
by Educational & Occupational Prestige (Male)

		English Proficiency		Use of English		Discarding Native Customs	
		F	sig.	F	sig.	F	sig.
Level of Education	1	16.62	.001	21.50	.001	2.42	NS
	2	7.84	.001	7.34	.001	.36	NS
	3	1.72	NS	.60	NS	.37	NS
Level of Occupational Prestige	1	15.53	.001	16.69	.001	2.65	NS
	2	5.79	.004	4.34	.010	.52	NS
	3	.41	NS	.018	NS	.95	NS

(1) Difference in mean scores of CA indices among the three categories of respondents by one-way analysis of variance.
(2) Difference in mean scores of the three indices among the three categories of respondents by analysis of covariance with the length of sojourn in the U.S. controlled for.
(3) Test of interaction effect by analysis of covariance.

Table 38. Distribution of the CA Mean Scores by Education and Occupational Prestige (Female)

		English Proficiency		Use of English		Discarding Native Customs	
		A	B	A	B	A	B
Level of Education	Higher Education in U.S.	8.27	8.28	7.46	7.52	6.54	6.57
	Higher Education in Korea	10.40	10.42	8.73	8.79	6.61	6.64
	No College Education	11.00	10.89	9.34	8.91	6.00	5.83
Level of Occupational Prestige	Professional	NS	NS	NS	NS	NS	NS
	Other White Collar	10.83	10.82	9.14	9.02	6.44	6.39
	Blue Collar	8.87	8.99	7.63	7.84	6.66	6.75

A: CA mean scores without the length of sojourn controlled.
B: CA mean scores with the length of sojourn controlled.

Table 39.   F Values and Significance Levels for CA Indices
by Educational and Occupational Prestige (Female)

		English Proficiency		Use of English		Discarding Native Customs	
		F	sig.	F	sig.	F	sig.
Level of Education	1	5.41	.007	2.13	NS	.44	NS
	2	5.16	.008	1.96	NS	.76	NS
	3	.84	NS	3.33	.05	.10	NS
Level of Occupational Prestige	1	14.04	.001	8.06	.006	.24	NS
	2	12.74	.001	5.50	.020	.61	NS
	3	.002	NS	.025	NS	.55	NS

(1) Difference in mean scores of CA indices among the three categories of respondents by one-way analysis of variance.
(2) Difference in mean scores of the three indices among the three categories of respondents by analysis of covariance with the length of sojourn in the U.S. controlled for.
(3) Test of interaction effect by analysis of covariance.

degree of cultural assimilation. Only exception is found in one
CA index (Discarding Native Customs).

Tables 38 and 39 provide information on the female respondents.
As previously indicated, the level of occupational prestige clas-
sifies them into two rather than three categories. These tables
yield findings similar to those for the male respondents (Tables
36 and 37), with one exception: among the three educational categories of the female respondents, the difference in the mean
scores for one CA index (the Use of English) is so reduced, after
the effect of the length of sojourn is controlled, that it is no
longer significant at the .05 level. At the same time, significant
interaction effect is observed in this index, suggesting no clear-
cut pattern.

In conclusion, Hypothesis 1 is confirmed for the male respondents with an exception, one CA index (Discarding Native Customs).
For the female respondents, however, the hypothesis is confirmed
only for the level of occupational prestige. As in the case of
the male respondents, one CA index (Discarding Native Customs)
is found to be insignificant for the females.

Hypothesis 2: Social assimilation is not
related to socio-economic status among Korean
immigrants.

If Hypothesis 2 is true, it should follow that both levels of
education and occupational prestige are not significantly
related to the SA scores. Table 40 presents the distribution

66

of male respondents in three categories by the levels of education and occupational prestige, their SA mean scores (A) and adjusted mean scores (B), and Table 41, three F values and significance levels associated with them. Contrary to our expectation, the level of education is positively related to the mean scores of the three SA indices. The F test shows that the differences in the mean scores of the three SA indices are significant at least at the .05 level.

When the effect of the length of residence in the U.S. is controlled, however, the difference in the mean scores of the three SA indices are so drastically reduced that the differences are no longer significant at the .05 level. Thus, Hypothesis 2 is confirmed by the level of education.

The results for the level of occupational prestige are similar to those for the level of education, with one exception: the level of occupational prestige is positively and significantly related to the scores of one SA index (Perceived Equal Treatment) even after the time variable is controlled.

Tables 42 and 43 present data on the female respondents. The two SES variables are significantly related to the mean scores of the three SA indices. This relationship remains unchanged in one SA index (Invitation by Americans) even after the time variable is controlled. The two SES variables are, however, neither positively nor significantly related to the scores of the remaining two SA indices, when the time variable is controlled.

Table 40. Distribution of the SA Mean Scores by Educational and Occupational Prestige (Male)

		Frequency of being invited		Frequency of inviting home		Equal Treatment	
		A	B	A	B	A	B
Level of Education	Higher Education in U.S.	3.90	2.42	3.30	2.27	6.27	5.64
	Higher Education in Korea	1.96	2.47	1.32	1.74	4.83	5.05
	No College Education	1.30	1.79	1.24	1.58	4.65	4.86
Level of Occupational Prestige	Professionals	4.30	3.36	3.25	2.45	6.15	5.69
	Other White Collar	2.84	2.62	2.15	1.96	5.58	5.47
	Blue Collar	1.12	1.72	1.00	1.51	4.38	4.67

A: SA mean scores without time factor controlled.
B: SA mean scores with time factor controlled.

Table 41. F Values and Significance Levels for SA Indices
by Educational and Occupational Prestige (Female)

		Frequency of being invited		Frequency of inviting home		Equal Treatment	
		F	sig.	F	sig.	F	sig.
Level of Education	1	6.07	.003	6.01	.004	8.49	.001
	2	.43	NS	.36	NS	1.13	NS
	3	.01	NS	.08	NS	.42	NS
Level of Occupational Prestige	1	10.38	.001	5.59	.005	10.73	.001
	2	2.37	NS	.79	NS	3.28	.040
	3	.09	NS	1.21	NS	.29	NS

(1) Difference in mean scores of SA indices among the
three categories of respondents by one-way analysis
of variance.
(2) Difference in mean scores of the three indices among
the three categories of respondents by analysis of
covariance with the length of sojourn in the U.S.
controlled for.
(3) Test of interaction effect by analysis of covariance.

Table 42. Distribution of SA Mean Scores by Educational and Occupational Prestige (Female)

		Invitation by * Americans		Invitation by ** Immigrants		Equal Treatment	
		A	B	A	B	A	B
Level of Education	Higher Education in U.S.	4.67	4.31	3.00	2.70	6.56	6.20
	Higher Education in Korea	1.92	1.97	1.55	1.60	5.47	5.53
	No College Education	1.27	1.33	1.64	1.68	5.00	5.06
Level of Occupational Prestige	Professionals	NS	NS	NS	NS	NS	NS
	Other White Collar	2.77	2.65	2.25	2.17	5.84	5.73
	Blue Collar	1.13	1.33	.87	1.03	5.00	5.20

A: SA mean scores without time variable controlled.
B: SA mean scores with time variable controlled.
* Invitation by Americans is the same as "Frequency of being invited."
** Invitation by Immigrants is the same as "Frequency of inviting home."

Table 43. F Values and Significance Levels for SA Indices by Educational and Occupational Prestige (Female)

		Invitation by* Americans		Invitation by** Immigrants		Equal Treatment	
		F	sig.	F	sig.	F	sig.
Level of Education	1	5.70	.006	1.26	NS	1.49	NS
	2	4.43	.010	.69	NS	.82	NS
	3	1.09	NS	3.33	.050	2.25	NS
Level of Occupational Prestige	1	6.49	.010	5.03	.030	2.83	NS
	2	4.45	.040	3.14	NS	1.09	NS
	3	.52	NS	.41	NS	.83	NS

(1) Difference in mean scores of SA indices among the three categories of respondents by one-way analysis of variance.
(2) Difference in mean scores of the three indices among the three categories of respondents by analysis of covariance with length of sojourn in the U.S. controlled for.
 * Invitation by Americans is the same as "Frequency of being invited."
** Invitation by Immigrants is the same as "Frequency of inviting home."

In conclusion, for the male respondents, Hypothesis 2 is generally confirmed with the time variable controlled. However, for the female respondents, it is confirmed only by two SA indices when the time variable is controlled.

<u>Hypothesis 3</u>: Status inconsistency affects the degree of both social and cultural assimilation of Korean immigrants.

Since income is excluded as a measure of SES in this research, analysis of status inconsistency can be carried out on the basis of education-occupation discrepancy. To test the hypothesis, the respondents were divided in two categories by level of present occupation: high occupation (professional and non-professional white-collar workers) and low occupation (blue-collar workers).

Due to the fact that only two respondents have obtained American degress and are employed as blue-collar workers, the education variables used here refer only to the levels of education received in Korea. For our purpose, the respondents were divided in two categories: high education (bachelor's degree) and low education (no bachelor's degree).

The above categorization excludes three types of the male respondents: those who are not employed, those who failed to indicate either their occupation or their level of education in Korea, and those who had not obtained a bachelor's degree in Korea but did obtain such a degree in the U.S. In addition, the female respondents are dropped from testing Hypothesis 3, because

72

there was only one respondent with low education and high occupation. Therefore, Hypothesis 3 is tested only for the male respondents.

Cross-classification by the levels of occupational prestige and education produces the following four types of male respondents: low education with low occupation (N=9), low education with high occupation (N=12), high education with low occupation (N=45), and high education with high occupation (N=64). On the basis of this classification, two objectively consistent groups are identified (low education with low occupation and high education with high occupation), and two objectively inconsistent groups (low education with high occupation and high education with low occupation).

Regardless of the level of education, those with high occupational prestige are found to have been in the U.S. for a longer period of time (5.55 years for low education and 5.51 years for high education) than those with low occupational prestige (2.41 years for low education and 3.31 years for high education). Moreover, the respondents' length of residence is linearly related to the degree of perceived status inconsistency, as will be shown later. From these findings, an interesting fact emerges with respect to the degree of perceived status inconsistency, which is measured by adding scores of three questions of perceived status inconsistency, ranging from three to fifteen points.

Contrary to our expectations, those with high occupational prestige are found to show higher scores of perceived status

73

inconsistency ($\bar{x}$ = 11.03) than those with low occupational prestige ($\bar{x}$ = 8.09), while the reverse is true in terms of the level
of education. Consequently, one objectively inconsistent group
characterized by high education with low occupation displays the
lowest score of perceived status inconsistency ($\bar{x}$ = 7.72), and
another objectively inconsistent group characterized by low education with high occupation shows the highest score ($\bar{x}$ = 11.43).
The two objectively consistent groups show intermediate scores
($\bar{x}$ = 9.50 and $\bar{x}$ = 10.99 respectively). Table 44 demonstrates
the above rank order.

Table 44. Distribution of Mean Scores of Perceived Inconsistency
Among the Four Types of the Male Respondents

	Low Education				High Education			
	Low Occupation		High Occupation		Low Occupation		High Occupation	
T.S.I.	Mean	S.D.	Mean	S.D.	Mean	S.D.	Mean	S.D.
	9.50	2.74	11.43	3.45	7.72	2.76	10.99	3.14

T.S.I.: Types of Status Inconsistency

To establish relationships between objective status inconsistency and assimilation indices, dummy variable regression
analysis was used. If status inconsistency affects the degree
of assimilation, only the two objectively inconsistent groups

74

will show significant difference between the observed and expected assimilation scores.*

Table 45 presents the observed and expected assimilation mean scores for the four groups of respondents, the difference between the two types of scores and the levels of significance. A significant discrepancy is observed between the observed and expected scores of the two CA indices (English Proficiency and Use of English) from two objectively consistent groups and one objectively inconsistent group (high education with low occupation). No significant discrepancy is, however, observed from another objectively inconsistent group (low education with high occupation). When significant differences are found from two objectively consistent groups, but not from an objectively inconsistent group, the differences cannot be attributed to the status inconsistency. With regard to the CA indices, therefore, no significant discrepancy between the observed and expected scores is found to be attributable to status inconsistency.

In the case of each of the two SA indices (Invitation by Americans, Invitation by Immigrants), the two objectively consistent groups demonstrate no significant difference, between the

---

* Using dummy-variable multiple regression equations, we assessed the effects of status inconsistencies on assimilation by comparing the observed assimilation levels with the theoretically expected levels. If the observed levels are greater than the expected ones, we can infer that a pure status inconsistency effect is operative. For a detailed discussion, see Treiman (1966: 659-660).

Table 45.   Observed and Expected CA and SA Mean Scores,
            Difference between the Scores, and Levels of
            Significance

		Low Education in Korea		High Education in Korea	
		Low Occupation in U.S. (12)	High Occupation in U.S. (9)	Low Occupation in U.S. (45)	High Occupation in U.S. (64)
English Proficiency	1	7.67	10.56	10.09	11.30
	2	9.92	11.40	8.27	9.75
	3	-2.25 *	-.84	1.82 *	1.55 *
Use of English	1	6.17	9.23	8.25	9.86
	2	8.11	9.95	6.69	8.53
	3	-1.94 *	-.72	1.56 *	1.33 *
Discarding Native Customs	1	5.67	6.23	6.25	6.85
	2	6.25	6.84	5.66	7.44
	3	-.58	-.61	.59	-.59
Invitations by Americans	1	.50	2.11	1.83	3.26
	2	1.25	3.22	.34	3.22
	3	-.75	-1.11	1.49 *	.04
Invitations by Immigrants	1	.75	1.44	1.08	2.40
	2	1.14	3.27	.52	2.35
	3	-.39	-1.83 *	.56	.05
Equal Treatment	1	4.25	4.89	4.36	5.79
	2	4.43	5.72	3.97	5.26
	3	-.18	-.83	.39	.53

*Significant at the .05 level by two-tailed test.
(1) Observed CA and SA mean scores.
(2) Expected CA and SA mean scores.
(3) The difference between two scores.

observed and expected scores, while the two objectively inconsistent groups do show significant difference. However, in one SA
index (Invitation by Immigrants), the observed score is smaller
than the expected score. It means that the effect of status
inconsistency operates only in another SA index (Invitation by
Americans). It is, therefore, concluded that Hypothesis is
confirmed only by one SA index.

> Hypothesis 4. There is no linear relationship between
> the length of residence in the United States and the
> degree of cultural and social assimilation among Korean
> immigrants.

To test Hypothesis 4, respondents were divided into five
categories of the length of residence: 1-2 years, 3-4 years,
5-6 years, 7-8 years, and 9 years or more.

The four tables (46, 47, 48, and 49) present the distribution of male and female respondents in the above five categories,
their (categories) SA and CA mean scores, values of eta square,
values of R square and F values, and the level of significance.

Among the five categories of male respondents, as their
length of residence in the U.S. increases, their SA and CA mean
scores increase correspondingly. A similar observation is made
regarding the five groups of female respondents, with the exception of one CA index (Willingness to Discard Native Customs) and
one SA index (Invitation by Americans). It is therefore main-
tained that both male and female respondents of the five categories,

77

with few exceptions, display a positive correlation between the length of residence in the U.S. and the SA and CA mean scores.

The above findings, however, do not provide any <u>direct evidence of a linear relationship</u> between the length of residence and the SA and CA scores. In order to test their linearity, values of eta square and R square were calculated. Both the values of eta square and R square measure the proportion of variance in the SA and CA scores which can be explained by the length of residence: the former explains both linear and non-linear variation, and the latter, linear variation only. When the difference between the values of eta square and R square is calculated and adjusted by their respective degree of freedom, the degree of departure from linearity can be obtained (See Tables 46 and 47).

For the male respondents, the difference between the values of eta square and R square is so small that the departure from linearity is not significant at the .05 level. This indicates that a linear relationship exists between the length of residence in the U.S. and each of the three SA indices.

With regard to CA indices the difference between the values of eta square and R square is again so small as to warrant non-linear relationship. However, the strength of the relationship between the length of residence and one CA index (Willingness to Discard Native Customs) is too weak, as demonstrated by the values of eta square and R sqaure, rendering the linear relationship for this variable meaningless. It indicates that a linear

Table 46. Distribution of SA Mean Scores by Length of Residence, Values of Eta Square and R Square, F Values, Levels of Significance Associated with them (Male).

Length of Residence	Invitation by Americans		Invitation by Immigrants		Equal Treatment	
	Mean	S.D.	Mean	S.D.	Mean	S.D.
1 - 2 (48)	.81	1.14	.51	1.38	4.24	1.50
3 - 4 (51)	1.96	3.24	1.49	2.25	4.81	1.60
5 - 6 (38)	3.23	4.59	1.76	2.70	5.27	1.81
7 - 8 (12	3.08	2.81	3.41	2.87	5.92	1.88
9 or more (19)	5.26	3.49	4.73	3.84	6.64	2.21
Eta Square	.16		.22		.15	
R Square	.15		.20		.14	
F Value	.45		1.04		.12	
Significance	.71		.37		.94	

Table 47. Distribution of CA Mean Scores by Length of
Residence, Values of Eta Square and R Square,
F Values, Levels of Significance Associated
with them (Male)

Length of Residence	English Proficiency		Use of English		Discarding Native Customs	
	Mean	S.D.	Mean	S.D.	Mean	S.D.
1 - 2 (48)	9.36	2.89	7.36	2.32	5.92	2.09
3 - 4 (51)	10.44	1.92	8.73	2.14	6.42	1.72
5 - 6 (38)	10.24	2.11	8.82	1.90	6.72	1.91
7 - 8 (12)	11.59	1.62	10.50	2.11	7.42	1.50
9 or more (19)	12.79	1.78	11.69	2.56	6.79	1.87
Eta Square	.17		.27		.04	
R Square	.15		.25		.03	
F Value	1.54		1.39		.71	
Significance	.20		.24		.54	

Table 48. Distribution of SA Mean Scores by Length of Residence, Values of Eta Square and R Square, F Values, Levels of Significance Associated with them (Female)

Length of Residence	Invitation by Americans		Invitation by Immigrants		Equal Treatment	
	Mean	S.D.	Mean	S.D.	Mean	S.D.
1 - 2 (29)	1.17	1.62	.89	1.44	4.80	1.61
3 - 4 (32)	1.82	1.79	1.84	2.51	4.85	1.70
5 - 6 (19)	1.42	1.89	.73	.80	5.11	1.79
7 - 8 (16)	2.87	3.26	1.87	2.77	6.63	2.63
9 or more (17)	4.35	3.46	4.00	3.88	7.00	1.45
Eta Square	.18		.16		.19	
R Square	.14		.90		.17	
F Value	1.56		3.21		1.30	
Significance	.20		.02		.27	

Table 49. Distribution of CA Mean Scores by Length of Residence, Values of Eta Square and R Square, F Values, Levels of Significance Associated with them (Female)

Length of Residence	English Proficiency		Use of English		Discarding Native Customs	
	Mean	S.D.	Mean	S.D.	Mean	S.D.
1 - 2 (29)	9.42	2.35	7.80	1.65	6.21	1.56
3 - 4 (32)	9.60	2.63	8.22	1.96	7.04	1.09
5 - 6 (19)	9.95	2.09	8.27	1.52	6.69	2.42
7 - 8 (16)	11.13	1.96	9.69	2.24	6.44	1.63
9 or more (17)	10.48	2.09	10.65	2.52	7.48	1.41
Eta Square	.06		.21		.07	
R Square	.04		.19		.02	
F Value	.64		1.05		1.71	
Significance	.59		.37		.16	

relationship exists between the length of residence and only two CA indices (English Proficiency and Use of English).

For the female respondents the difference between the values of eta square and R square is small only in the cases of two SA indices (Invitation by Americans and Perceived Equal Treatment). The length of residence is therefore linearly related to these two SA indices. However, for the third SA index (Invitation by Immigrants) no linear relationship is found. (See Tables 48 and 49).

The values of eta square and R square indicate that the strength of the relationship between the length of residence and two CA indices (English Proficiency and Willingness to Discard Native Customs) is so weak as to establish any kind of relationship. However, the difference between the values of eta square for the CA index (Use of English) is significant to warrant linear relationship.

In summary, for the male respondents the length of residence in the U.S. is linearly related to the three SA indices and two of the three CA indices. For the female respondents, length of residence is linearly related to two SA indices and one CA index. Thus, Hypothesis 4 is generally rejected for the male respondents and partially confirmed among female respondents.

C. Summary and Discussion

In the test of hypotheses, the length of residence in the U.S. emerges as a critical variable which is highly correlated with other variables. This necessitates to use it as a major control variable. Since the time factor is a pervasive variable in analyzing all hypotheses and deals most directly with Hypothesis 4, the results of hypotheses testing will be discussed in the following order Hypothesis 4, 1, 2, and 3.

As measured by Pearsonian correlation coefficients, the length of residence in the U.S. is highly correlated with the CA and SA indices. Moreover, the length of residence is generally linearly related to all assimilation indices for the male respondents. Therefore, Hypothesis 4 which predicting a non-linear relationship between the time variable, is rejected for the male respondents. For the female respondents, however, the length of residence is linearly related to part of the assimilation indices.

The test of Hypothesis 4 suggests three points which deserve judicious review. First, it identifies the assimilation indices which are positively affected by the length of residence in the U.S. Some of the indices are so identified among both the male and female respondents: Invitation by American, Perceived Equal Treatment and the Use of English. This means that as the length of respondents' residence in the U.S. increases, the following two things take place among the respondents regardless of sex: (1) they are invited by Americans more frequently and perceive an increasing degree of equal treatment, and (2) they subscribe to a greater number of American newspapers and magazines and use English more frequently at home.

84

Second, with regard to other two assimilation indices

(Invitation by Immigrants, and English Proficiency) the time

variable is only related to the male respondents. The findings

indicate that sex differences do exist in some dimensions of

social and cultural assimilation. One of such dimensions is

English Proficiency. In contrast to the male respondents, no

positive relationship is found among the female respondents,

meaning that the increase in the length of residence does not

improve their English Proficiency.

Another sex difference is found in the frequency of invita-

tion extended by the immigrants. Unlike the case of the male

respondents, the length of residence does not increase the

frequency of invitation by immigrants among the female respondents.

This shows that the female respondents fail to match the frequency

of invitation extended by Americans with that of invitation ex-

tended by the immigrants themselves. This would seem to suggest

that the females face more difficulties than males in social

assimilation because of their failure to reciprocate favors. One

may wonder whether this differential stems from the traditional

sex role and power structure of immigrants' families.

Third, the length of residence is linearly related to more

assimilation indices for the male respondents than for the female

respondents. This suggests that as the length of residence in-

creases, the male respondents are more pervasively assimilated

than the female respondents.

Hypothesis 1 is confirmed for the male respondents with exception of one CA index (Willingness to Discard Native Customs).
For the female respondents, the above hypothesis is similarly
confirmed by the level of occupational prestige. This reveals
that the SES variables are not related in any meaningful way to
the Willingness to Discard Native Customs among the respondents
of both sexes.

Hypothesis 2 is generally confirmed for the male respondents,
but partly for the female respondents, when the time variable is
controlled. This unequivocally demonstrates that the SES variables
exert no influence on the degree of social assimilation for the
male respondents while this is partly true for the female respondents. One may question whether this difference would mean that
Korean males are less socially accepted by Americans than Korean
females regardless of the level of SES, even though Korean males
reciprocate favor (invitation extended by Americans) better than
Korean females.

Hypothesis 3 is generally rejected for the male respondents:
however, the effect of status inconsistency is found to be related
to one SA index. Of particular note is that their objective SES
of the male respondents does not seem to affect directly their
perceived status inconsistency. If the degree of subjectively
perceived status inconsistency reflects their objective SES, the
objectively inconsistent groups should show a high score of perceived status inconsistency. This is, however, not true for one

86

objectively consistent group (high education with low occupation).
This raises important questions as to why their perceived status
inconsistency does not closely reflect their objectively apparent
status inconsistency.

As a final note, caution should be exercised in understanding
the expressions, "a higher degree of assimilation" and "increase
in the degree of assimilation" that are frequently used in this
paper. They are used to describe the relative degree of assimilation achieved by the respondents. By no means are they to be
construed as indicating that a category of respondents has made
satisfactory progress in the degree of assimilation. This is
particularly true with respect to the degree of social assimilation.

In fact, the great majority of the respondents show an extremely low degree of social assimilation. As already discussed
above, very few Koreans (3.2%) attend American churches, and none
is affiliated with any other American social organizations. Furthermore, about half of the respondents (52%) were either never
invited by Americans into their homes or did so only once. The
findings regarding the test of the four hypotheses should be under-
stood in this context.

Obviously, one of the reasons for the generally low degree
of social assimilation is the time factor. Since the majority of
them came to this country only recently, they have not had time
to achieve higher degree of social assimilation. As found in the
test of Hypothesis 4, they would achieve a higher degree of social

Table 50. Distribution of Mean Scores of Perceived
Status Inconsistency by Length of Residence
and Sex

Length of Residence in the U.S.	Scores of Perceived Status Inconsistency			
	Male Respondents		Female Respondents	
	N	Mean	N	Mean
1 - 2	34	9.92	19	9.22
3 - 4	43	9.05	20	10.05
5 - 6	30	9.50	13	12.47
7 - 8	11	10.91	12	13.00
9 or more	14	12.14	11	9.53
Eta Square	.08		.18	
R Square	.06		.04	
F Value	.92		4.13	
Significance	.43		.009	

assimilation as the length of their residence in the U.S. extends. In this respect, some optimism can be expressed. It is, however, doubtful that their progress will continue indefinitely.

An indication sustaining this doubt comes from the findings on perceived status inconsistency. As the length of residence increases up to the sixth year, the status inconsistency scores remain relatively stable but from the seventh year on the scores increase quite noticeably among the male respondents. Among the female respondents the scores increase up to the eighth year and then drop thereafter (Table 50). The above findings seem to suggest the time factor may have an adverse effect on the level of assimilation at a certain point in time because the increased perception of status inconsistency may reduce motivation for assimilation.

V. CONCLUSION AND IMPLICATIONS

Our project started with a general basic research inquiry:
how do the Korean immigrants in the Chicago Area adjust themselves
to the American way of life? Specifically, our main purpose for
this study was to analyze the differential patterns of cultural
and social assimilation of the immigrants as related to structural
variables (e.g., age, sex, marital status, type of residence,
occupation, religious affiliation, length of sojourn, etc.) In
addition to description and analysis of data, we expected to
generate some new theoretical insight for further empirical
research and possibly also social policy implications for promot-
ing interethnic relations.

In order to answer and meet the above inquiry and purpose,
our study was designed on two levels: descriptive and analytical.
On the descriptive level, we examined demographic characteristics,
socio-economic status, cultural adaptation and social assimilation
patterns, and general problem areas in adjustment. On the analytical level, a series of hypotheses were tested to analyze the
relationship between structural variable and the differential
degrees of cultural and social assimilation.

The detailed results of our findings need not be repeated
here. A cursory sketch of the most significant findings are,
however, summarized below for conclusive interpretation and
theoretical relevance.

The Korean immigrants are relatively young (median age of 36), most of them are married, highly educated (four years of college or more), and have been residing in Chicago less than six years (mean: 4.47 years). While 65 per cent of our sample held white-collar occupations at the time of their emigration from Korea, only 37 per cent currently hold the same level of occupation.

About half of our sample experience language difficulty and do not subscribe to any American printed media. For the majority of the respondents the traditional Korean food is predominantly preferred over Western food, while the latter is occasionally used for convenience. Membership in voluntary organization is largely limited to Korean ethnic organizations, with Korean churches dominating. Concerning social interaction with Americans, more than half of our sample do not have any American friends. While approximately one-third of the immigrants have never been invited by Americans, almost half of them have never invited Americans, indicating more immigrants have been invited by Americans than vice versa.

From the above descriptive sketch of objective dimensions one could infer that most of the immigrants in the Chicago area are in the very early stage of adaptation process, having the "usual" adjustment difficulties, such as language, underemployment, housing, social distance, marginality, etc. Feelings of ambivalence, status inconsistency, and identity problem among the immigrants are thus likely to be observed. The feelings of ambivalence

91

are evident in their attitudes toward their cultural and social identity: for instance, the majority of our sample agree that some Korean customs should be discarded, such as the burden of traditional family obligations, male-dominant marital roles, authoritarian treatment of children, ancestor worship, cumbersome Korean cookery, and expensive wedding and other traditional ceremonies. In contrast to the above, however, the vast majority of our sample indicated that Korean language, history, morals, and general customs should be taught to their children. These seemingly contradictory findings reveal the immigrants' ambivalence between their desire to discard some specific aspects of traditional culture and desire to preserve their general ethnic heritage through generations. The immigrants' ambivalent feelings are also manifest in other areas. Although the majority of our sample are reserved or negative about living with Americans as their neighbors, making friends with Americans, and interracial marriage, the overwhelming majority indicate their wish for their children to associate with American children and feel favorable toward the Anglicization of their first names.

However, despite objectively apparent status inconsistency (the high pre-immigration educational attainment versus low post-immigration status), nearly half of our sample perceive little status inconsistency, about half of them feel most Americans accept them as their equals, and the majority of them think that they are not discriminated against in terms of monetary remuneration for their work. A plausible explanation for the attitudinal

92

ambivalence and perceptual incongruency seems to be that the respondents, being newcomers, are not yet able to grasp the reality which belies them: the relatively high standard of living they enjoy in the U.S. in comparison to that in Korea may tend to prevent any sense of relative deprivation from entering their consciousness in the early years of their immigrant life. This would mean the recent Korean immigrants have not yet transferred their reference groups from Korean peers to WASP peers. This may be why only small portion of our sample (6.2%) cited inadequate income as the most important problem. Our respondents' perception of their adjustment problem in order of importance is language, busy routine, concern for children, social isolation, job-related areas, inadequate income, and racial discrimination.

Whether this unrealistic perception of reality ("false consciousness") will continue is a moot question. As the immigrants' life conditions gradually improve, accompanied by raised levels of aspirations, they may tend to transfer their reference groups from Korean peers to WASP peers. When and if these phenomena occur, the immigrants may begin to experience feelings of relative deprivation and social marginality. Through our study such a conjecture cannot be verified. Our sample was inadequate to test the above proposition due to the fact that the majority of them arrived in the U.S. after 1970. It can be tested in Hawaii, Los Angeles, or New York where a substantial number of Korean immigrants have resided for a longer period.

Beyond the descriptive analysis we tested four hypotheses in order to examine existing theories and propositions through inductive generalizations. Each hypothesis contains assimilation variables relating them to various structural variables, especially sex and the length of sojourn.

The first hypothesis was derived from Weinstock's and Silver's proposition that the higher the socio-economic status, the higher the degree of cultural assimilation will be. The above proposition is generally confirmed for both sexes. The second hypothesis was again mainly based on Gordon's "acculturation only" typology that socio-economic status may have little or no direct effect upon the degree of social assimilation, although it may be related to cultural assimilation (as was confirmed in our second hypothesis). This hypothesis is generally confirmed for the male respondents, but partly for the female respondents. This difference in the strength of confirmation of the above hypothesis generates an interesting question: are Korean males less socially accepted by Americans than Korean females regardless of the level of socio-economics status?

The third hypothesis was derived from our impression of the unique characteristics of the recent Korean "elite immigrants" (high preimmigrantion educational and occupational status). Using the existing theories of status inconsistency (e.g., Lenski, Treiman, Olsen and Tully), we hypothesized that pre- and post-immigration status inconsistency affects the degree of social and cultural assimilation. Implied in this proposition is an assumption

94

that the feelings of relative deprivation would hinder the immigrants' rapid assimilation into American culture and society.
Our data, however, generally do not give strong support to the
hypothesis. Moreover, the immigrants' subjectively perceived
status inconsistency does not closely correspond to objectively
apparent status inconsistency (e.g., those with high education
and low occupation show generally low scores of perceived status
inconsistency). Is this a manifestation of "false consciousness,"
mentioned earlier? We must again defer the discussion on this
question until later.

Our last hypothesis was formulated based on the assumption:
although the process of assimilation may progress to a point, in
parallel with the initial adjustment period and subsequent upward
occupational mobility with increased desire for Anglo-conformity,
such progress may not continue beyond a certain temporal point,
when the "successful" immigrant starts to compare his life-chances
to those of his WASP peers. We hypothesized, therefore, the
relationship between the length of sojourn and the degree of
cultural and social assimilation may not be linear. Contrary to
our expectation, the above hypothesis is rejected for the male
respondents. For the female respondents, however, the hypothesis
is confirmed only for certain dimensions of assimilation (English
Proficiency, Invitation by Immigrants, and Willingness to Discard
Native Customs). These findings clearly demonstrate the existence
of sex differences in the dimensions of assimilations as related
to the length of residence in the U.S.

95

The most plausible interpretation of the findings for the male respondents would be that either the male immigrants are making real progress toward total structural assimilation ("the keystone of the arch of assimilation" in Gordon's terms) into American culture and society as time lapses, or are just passing through a temporary adaptation stage with "false" or "naive" definition of their situation. Such a situation may lead to an identification crisis sooner or later when the immigrants begin to "discover" an immutable barrier ("race") that would block their way toward structural assimilation.

As mentioned earlier, it is impossible to justify either of the above interpretations on the Korean immigrants in the Chicago area without a longitudinal study in the future. The present study, however, has some theoretical, methodological, and practical implications.

As discussed earlier in this conclusion, our respondents revealed their seemingly mixed feelings on many crucial assimilation items, such as discarding native traditional customs versus preservation of ethnic identity, reservation about making friends with Americans versus favorable attitude towards the Anglicization of Korean names, reservation about living with Americans as their neighbors versus favorable attitude toward their children to associate with American children, and objectively apparent underemployment versus little subjective perception of relative deprivation. Since these various dimensions of the respondents' cognitive inconsistency might have seeped in their responses in various ways, the relationships among the assimilation variables have become extremely complicated. Nevertheless, such ambivalence reflected in our data is very significant for a processual analysis of the immigrants' adaptation process.

Our theoretical contention is that the immigrants' cognitive ambivalence is closely related to the time variable. In other words, our respondents may be going through one of several critical phases or stages in the adaptation process. A hypothetical mode for adaptation process is constructed to explicate our contention (see Figure 1).

Our respondents may be going through the "resolution stage" - between exigency and optimum stages - in our processual model shown in Figure 1. At this stage most of the immigrants' initial exigent conditions (e.g., culture shock, underemployment, language barrier, social isolation, etc.) may have already been redressed through their familiarity with American culture, employment (even though some of them may be underemployed), improvement in English proficiency, and relatively stable incomes. Although some of their initial adjustment difficulties may still linger on, the immigrants may have now developed a taste for material affluence (purchasing a color T.V., a new car, a house, etc.), their interaction with Americans may increase, desire for Anglo-conformity may also increase (conversion to Christianity and Anglicization of names), and thus a degree of cultural assimilation may progress as time goes on.

Figure 1:   Critical Phases in Adaptation Process:
A Hypothetical Model

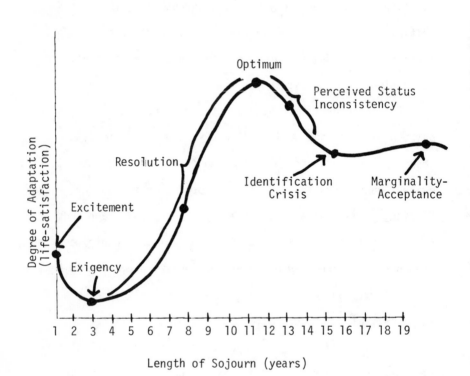

Despite this progressive acculturation and relatively improved life conditions, the immigrants seem to find themselves psychologically in the middle between Korea and America. Their reference groups still seem to be the Koreans "back home" and/or Korean-Americans in the U.S. No wonder most of our respondents perceive little sense of relative deprivation, in spite of their objectively apparent status inconsistency. To put it simply, the immigrants, at this stage of adaptation process, would feel rather comfortable by identifying themselves with Korean peers than with WASP peers. Although their aspirations for further "success" in the U.S. become accentuated, the immigrants may still perceive themselves as "guests" who cannot possibly enter the intimate social circle (Gemeinschaft) of their "hosts." Moreover, the idea of competing against the dominant groups of their host society would be unrealistic - at least in their own generation.

The above interpretation may explain the immigrants' cognitive ambivalence which affects their differential adjustment patterns. How would the immigrants resolve their cognitive ambivalence? Our hypothetical processual model may be able to answer the question and to predict the direction and intensity of the immigrants' comfort and plight; however, that is beyond the scope of the present research (cf. Hurh, 1977).

Finally, the practical implications concern the possible application of our findings to the improvement of Korean immigrants' life conditions in particular, and the interethnic relations in the U.S. in general. The results of our study reveal most of the Korean immigrants in the Chicago area seem to adjust themselves to American culture progressively, mainly due to their high levels of education and achievement motive. On the other hand, however, they are undergoing cognitive ambivalence, mainly due to their limited range of social assimilation. As in the case of other immigrants, the Korean immigrants' adaptation to their host society is a dialectical process; the interplay between the structure of their host society and the subjective definition of the immigrants' situation in a temporal nexus.

The above notion implies that the immigrants' "comfort and plight" ambivalence may eventually lead to a severe identity crisis which in turn would result in voluntary ethnic segregation, when and if the majority members of American society maintain social distance from the immigrants. Under this condition, any governmental policies based on the ideas of "Anglo-conformity" and "melting pot," or even "assimilation" would be meaningless, unless they are directed toward reducing or eliminating social (structural) barrier between the WASP and the immigrants, especially non-white immigrants (cf. Hurh, 1977).

REFERENCES

Becker, Tamar
  1968 "Patterns of attitudinal changes among foreign students."
        American Journal of Sociology 73 (January): 431-442.

Bogardus, Emory S.
  1968 "Comparing racial distance in Ethiopia, South Africa, and
        the United States." Sociology and Social Research 52
        (January): 149-156.

Cha, Marn J.
  1975 "Ethnic political orientation as function of assimilation:
        with reference to Koreans in Los Angeles." Journal of
        Korean Affairs 5: 14-25.

Glazer, Nathan
  1954 "Ethnic groups in America: from national culture to
        ideology." Pp. 158-173 in M. Berger et al (eds.), Free-
        dom and Control in Modern Society. New York: Octagon Books.

Goffman, Irwin
  1957 "Status inconsistency and preference for change in power
        distribution." American Sociological Review 22 (June):
        275-281.

Goldstein, Sidney and Calvin Goldscheider
  1968 Jewish Americans. Englewood Cliffs, New Jersey: Prentice-
        Hall.

Gordon, Milton
  1964 Assimilation in American Life. New York: Oxford.

The Hankook Ilbo Miju News
  1975 "Chicago haninun 2,500 myong?" The Hankook Ilbo Miju News,
        August 14.

Hodge, Robert W., Donald J. Treiman, and Peter H. Rossi
  1966 "A comparative study of occupational prestige." Pp. 309-
        321 in R. Bendix and S. Lipset (eds.), Class, Status and
        Power: Social Stratification in Comparative Perspective.
        New York: Free Press.

Hsu, Francis L. K.
  1971 The Challenge of the American Dream: The Chinese in the
        United States. Belmont, California: Wadsworth.

Hurh, Won M.
   1977   Comparative Study of Korean Immigrants in the United States:
          A Typological Approach. San Francisco, California: R and
          E Research Associates, Inc.

Jade
   1975   "Korean Influx." Jade (December) 1: 22-23.

The Joong-ang Daily News
   1976   "Bǒonyǒng hanǔn jeiui Seoul." (The Prosperous Second
          Seoul). The Joong-ang Daily News (February 6).

Kang, T. S.
   1971   "Name change and acculturation." Pacific Sociological
          Review 14 (October): 403-412.

Kim, Bok-Lim C.
   1972   "Casework with Japanese and Korean wives of Americans."
          Social Casework 53 (May): 273-279.

Kim, Bok-Lim C. and Margaret E. Condon
   1975   "A study of Asian Americans in Chicago: their socio-economic
          characteristics, problems and service needs," Interim
          Report to the National Institute of Mental Health, U.S.
          Department of Health, Education and Welfare.

Kim, Hyung-chan
   1974   "Some aspects of social demography of Korean Americans."
          International Migration Review 8: 23-42.

Kim, Warren K.
   1971   Koreans in America. Seoul: Po Chin Chai.

Kitano, Harry L.
   [1969]   Japanese Americans: The Evolution of a Subculture. Engle-
   1976   wood Cliffs, New Jersey: Prentice-Hall.

Kitano, Harry L. and Stanley Sue
   1973   "The model minorities." The Journal of Social Issues 29:
          1-9.

Lenski, Gerhard
   1954   "Status crystalization: a non-vertical dimension of social
          status." American Sociological Review 19 (August) 405-413.
   1964   "Comment." Public Opinion Quarterly 28 (June): 326-330.

Lyman, Stanford M.
   1974   Chinese Americans. New York: Random House.

Merton, Robert, and Robert Nisbet
   1966   Contemporary Social Problems. New York: Harcourt, Brace.

Nelson, Edward E.
  1973 "Status inconsistency: its objective and subjective compo-
        nents." Sociological Quarterly (Winter): 3-18.

Olsen, Marvin E. and Judy C. Tully
  1972 "Socioeconomic-ethnic status inconsistency and preference
        for political change." American Sociological Review 37
        (October): 560-574.

Petersen, William
  1971 Japanese Americans. New York: Random House.

Rosenthal, Erich
  1960 "Acculturation without assimilation." American Journal of
        Sociology 66: 275-288.

Senter, Donovan
  1945 "Acculturation among New Mexican villages in comparison to
        adjustment patters of other Spanish-speaking Americans."
        Rural Sociology 10: 31-47.

Silvers, Ronald J.
  1965 "Structure and values in the explanation of acculturation
        rates." British Journal of Sociology 16 (March): 68-79.

Simpson, George E. and J. Milton Yinger
  1972 Racial and Cultural Minorities: An Analysis of Prejudice
        and Discrimination. New York: Harper and Row.

Stehr, N.
  1968 "Status inconsistency: the theoretical concept and its
        empirical referent." Pacific Sociological Review 11
        (Fall): 95-99.

Suits, D. B.
  1957 "Use of dummy-variables in regression equations." Journal
        of the American Statistical Association 52 (December):
        548-551.

Treiman, Donald J.
  1966 "Status discrepancy and prejudice." American Journal of
        Sociology 71 (May): 651-664.

U.S. Department of Health, Education, and Welfare
  1974 A Study of Selected Socio-Economic Characteristics of
        Ethnic Minorities based on the 1970 Census. Volume II:
        Asian Americans. Washington, D.C.: U.S. Government
        Printing Office.

U.S. Department of Justice
  1971-1974 Annual Report, Immigration and Naturalization Service.
            Washington, D.C.: U.S. Government Printing Office.

Weinstock, S. Alexander
  1963 "Role elements: a link between acculturation and occupa-
        tional status." British Journal of Sociology 14: 144-149.

Yoshihara, Nancy
  1976 "Koreans find riches, faded dreams in Los Angeles." Los
        Angeles Times (February 1), Part IV.

Yuan, D. Y.
  1963 "Voluntary segregation: a study of New York Chinatown."
        Phylon (Fall): 255-265.

APPENDIX

A. Cultural Assimilation Questionnaire

1. How well do you speak English?

> (1) Fluent
> (2) Good
> (3) Fair
> (4) Poor
> (5) Not at all

2. How well do you read English?

> (1) Fluent
> (2) Good
> (3) Fair
> (4) Poor
> (5) Not at all

3. How well do you write English?

> (1) Fluent
> (2) Good
> (3) Fair
> (4) Poor
> (5) Not at all

4. Do you subscribe to any American newspaper(s)?

> (1) Three or more
> (2) Two
> (3) One
> (4) None

If you do, what is/are its name(s)?

5. What section of your paper do you favor the most?

> (1) Political
> (2) Economic
> (3) Cultural
> (4) Sports
> (5) Advertisement
> (6) Comics
> (7) Other

6. Do you subscribe to any American magazine(s)? (Please exclude occupation related magazines).

    (1) Three or more
    (2) Two
    (3) One
    (4) None

If you do, what is/are its name(s)?

7. How frequently do you speak English at home?

    (1) Always
    (2) Frequently
    (3) Occasionally
    (4) Never

8. How do you feel about Koreans changing their names to American names?

    (1) Strongly approve
    (2) Moderately approve
    (3) Undecided
    (4) Moderately disapprove
    (5) Strongly disapprove

Please give reasons for feeling as you do.

9. How often do you use Western food? (Please check one of the following choices for breakfast, lunch and dinner)

    (1) Always
    (2) Frequently
    (3) Occasionally
    (4) Never

10. Do you think some of our customs should no longer be practiced because they delay acceptance of Koreans in to American society?

    (1) Strongly agree
    (2) Moderately agree
    (3) Undecided
    (4) Moderately disagree
    (5) Strongly disagree

If you agree, what specific customs should no longer be practiced in your opinion?

11. Do you think Korean language, history, morals, and customs should be taught to your children?

     (1) Strongly agree
     (2) Moderately agree
     (3) Undecided
     (4) Moderately disagree
     (5) Strongly disagree

B. Social Assimilation Questionnaire

1. Are you a member of any voluntary organizations, such as club or church? (Please exclude professional or trade organizations)

   If yes, what are the name(s) of organization(s)?

2. Would you feel more comfortable to live in predominantly American neighborhood than Korean?

   (1) Definitely yes
   (2) Probably yes
   (3) Undecided
   (4) Probably no
   (5) Definitely no

3. Do you think Americans easier to make friends with than Koreans?

   (1) Definitely yes
   (2) Probably yes
   (3) Undecided
   (4) Probably no
   (5) Definitely no

4. Do you have any close American friends in whom you can confide your personal problems?

   (1) Four or more
   (2) Three
   (3) Two
   (4) One
   (5) None

5. Do you feel most Americans accept you as thier equal?

   (1) Definitely yes
   (2) Probably yes
   (3) Undecided
   (4) Probably no
   (5) Definitely no

6. Would you say it is better for your children to play with American children than with Korean children, if circumstances allow?

   (1) Definitely yes
   (2) Probably yes
   (3) Undecided
   (4) Probably no
   (5) Definitely no

7. What do you think of interracial marriage between Koreans and Americans?

      (1) Strongly approve
      (2) Moderately approve
      (3) Undecided
      (4) Moderately disapprove
      (5) Strongly disapprove

8. Do you plan to retire in Korea?

      (1) Definitely yes
      (2) Probably yes
      (3) Undecided
      (4) Probably no
      (5) Definitely no

9. How often have you been invited by Americans to their homes in the past year? (Please exclude business-related ones)

      (1) 10 or more times
      (2) 7-9 times
      (3) 5-6 times
      (4) 3-4 times
      (5) 2 times
      (6) Once
      (7) Never

10. How often have you invited Americans to your home in the past year?

      (1) 10 or more times
      (2) 7-9 times
      (3) 5-6 times
      (4) 3-4 times
      (5) 2 times
      (6) Once
      (7) Never

11. Do you have any close Korean friends in whom you can confide your personal problems?

      (1) Four or more
      (2) Three
      (3) Two
      (4) One
      (5) None

C. <u>Questionnaire on Status Inconsistency and Perception of</u>
   <u>Opportunities in the United States</u>

1. Do you think your present income is comparable to that of your fellow workers?

   (1) Definitely yes
   (2) Probably yes
   (3) Don't know
   (4) Probably no
   (5) Definitely no

2. Do you think your present income is commensurate with the educational level you have achieved?

   (1) Definitely yes
   (2) Probably yes
   (3) Don't know
   (4) Probably no
   (5) Definitely no

3. Do you think your present occupation is commensurate with the educational level you have achieved?

   (1) Definitely yes
   (2) Probably yes
   (3) Don't know
   (4) Probably no
   (5) Definitely no

4. Generally speaking, do you think there are chances for you "to make it" in the United States, if you work hard enough?

   (1) Definitely yes
   (2) Probably yes
   (3) Don't know
   (4) Probably no
   (5) Definitely no

D. Questionnaire on Socio-Economic and Demographic Characteristics

1. Sex: Male   Female   (Please circle one)

2. Age:

3. Marital Status: Single   Married   Divorced   Other
   (Please circle one)

4. Family Members (cohabitating): (Please give their ages,
   occupations, if any, specifying whether they are full-time or
   part-time, and relations)

5. Date of Arrival in the United States:

6. Date of Arrival in Chicago:

7. Type of Residence: Own   Renting   Apartment   Other
   (Please circle one)

8. The highest educational level achieved in Korea:

9. The final occupation held in Korea: (Please specify the nature
   of work)

10. The highest educational level achieved in the United States:

11. Annual income in Korea at the time of emigration: (including
    regular annual salary, secondary income and others)

12. Current annual income in the United States: (including regular
    annual salary, secondary income and others)

E. Questionnaire on Commitment to Church Activities

1. Are you affiliated with any church? If you are, what church
   do you attend?

2. How often have you attended church services in the past year?

        (1) Every week
        (2) About twice a month
        (3) Once a month
        (4) About four to five times a year

3. In addition to attending regular church services, do you parti-
   cipate in other church activities? If so, what are the activities?

4. Did you attend church when you were in Korea? If so, how often?

     (1) Every week
     (2) About twice a month
     (3) Once a month
     (4) About four to five times a year

     What church did you attend? (Please give its name)

5. What are the different types of satisfaction you derive from attending church? What about dissatisfaction?

6. What is (or was) your parents' religious affiliation?

7. What was your grandparents' religious affiliation?

F.   Problem Areas in Adjustment

1. What are difficulties and/or problems you encounter today living in the United States? (Please state freely)

G.   Interviewer's Observations and Comments

1975 년 10 월

_____ 귀 하

미국 보건사회부 (Department of Health, Education & Welfare) 의 원조와 현재 저희들이 교편을 잡고있는 (Western Illinois University) 의 협조를 얻어 시카고에 거주하시는 한인교포들의 문화 및 사회적 적응관계를 연구코저 교포 전체중 약 500명을 무작위 추출로 선정 했는데 귀하의 가족의 한사람이 그중의 일원으로 포함됐읍니다.

이 연구의 목적은 어떤 특수 개인을 조사하고저 하는 것이 아니라 시카고 주위 한인교포 전체의 동향과 애로, 문제 사항등을 파악하는데 있읍니다. 이 견구 결과는 한인 교포의 복지를 위한 사업에 기본자료가 될것입니다.

바쁘실줄 아오나 저희들의 연구원이 귀하의 댁을 멀지 않아 방문하여 면담할 예정이오니 교포전체의 복지를 위해 적극 협력해 주시면 대단히 감사하겠읍니다.

허 원 무, 사회학 박사

김 혜 주, 사회학 박사

김 광 정, 사회학 박사

113

설 문 서

A. 문화적 동화에 대한 질문

1. 영어회화에 얼마나 능통하십니까?

    (1) 유창히 한다. (fluent) _____
    (2) 어느정도 잘 한다. (good) _____
    (3) 그저 그렇다 (fair) _____
    (4) 잘 못 한다. (poor) _____
    (5) 전혀 못 한다. (not at all) _____

2. 영어로 읽으시는데 얼마나 능숙하십니까?

    (1) 아주 잘 읽는다. _____
    (2) 어느정도 잘 읽는다. _____
    (3) 그저 그렇다. _____
    (4) 잘 못 읽는다. _____
    (5) 전혀 못 읽는다. _____

3. 영어로 글을 쓰는데 얼마나 능숙하십니까?

    (1) 아주 잘 쓴다. _____
    (2) 어느 정도 잘 쓴다. _____
    (3) 그저 그렇다. _____
    (4) 잘 못 쓴다. _____
    (5) 전혀 못 쓴다. _____

4. 영어 신문을 구독하십니까?

    (1) 세가지 또는 그 이상 _____
    (2) 두가지 _____
    (3) 한가지 신문을 구독한다. _____
    (4) 아니다. _____

    구독하시면 그 신문의 이름은?

_____

5. 구독하신다면 어느면을 주로 읽으십니까?

    (1) 정치 _____ (2) 경제 _____ (3) 문화 _____
    (4) 운동 _____ (5) 광고 _____ (6) 만화 _____
    (7) 기타 _____ (8) 어느면이고 별로 읽지않는다. _____

6. 영어 잡지를 구독하십니까? (학술 및 기술잡지는 제외)

   (1) 세가지 또는 그 이상 _____
   (2) 두가지 _____
   (3) 한가지 _____
   (4) 아니다. _____

7. 구독하신다면 그 잡지의 이름은?

_____

_____

8. 집에서 가족끼리 영어를 하십니까?

   (1) 항상한다. _____   (2) 자주한다. _____
   (3) 가끔한다. _____   (4) 전혀 안한다. _____

9. 한국 이름을 미국 이름으로 고치는 것을 어떻게 생각하십니까?

   (1) 전적으로 찬성 _____
   (2) 어느정도 찬성 _____
   (3) 모르겠다. _____
   (4) 어느정도 불찬성 _____
   (5) 전적으로 불찬성 _____

   왜 그렇게 생각하시는지요. (자유로운 답변)

_____

_____

10. 양식을 어느정도 하십니까?

  a. 아침: (1) 항상한다 ____ (2) 자주한다 ____ (3) 가끔한다 ____ (4) 전혀 안한다
  b. 점심: (1) ____ (2) ____ (3) ____ (4) ____
  c. 저녁: (1) ____ (2) ____ (3) ____ (4) ____

11. 현재 미국에서 생활하시는데 지장을 주는 한국풍습은 버려야
   한다고 생각하십니까?

   (1) 전적으로 찬성 _____   (2) 어느정도 찬성 _____
   (3) 모르겠다 _____   (4) 어느정도 불찬성 _____
   (5) 전적으로 불찬성 _____

12. 찬성하신다면 특히 어떤 풍습을 버려야 한다고 생각하십니까?
   (자유로운 대답) _____

_____

_____

_____

13. 자녀에게 한국말, 역사, 도덕, 기타 풍습을 가르켜야 된다고
    생각 하십니까?

    (1) 전적으로 찬성 _____   (2) 어느정도 찬성 _____
    (3) 모르겠다 _____   (4) 어느정도 불찬성 _____
    (5) 전적으로 불찬성 _____

14. 찬성하신다면 어느면을 더 강조하고 싶으신지요 ?
    순위로 열거 해주십시오.

    _____

    _____

15. 가장 흥미있게 보시는 테레비(TV) 프로그램은 무엇입니까?

    _____   _____

    _____   _____

B. 사회적 동화에 대한 질문서

    1. 어느 크럽이나 교회같은 사회조직체의 회원으로 계십니까?
       (직업적이나 학술적 기관은 제외)
       만일 회원이시라면 그 조직체의 이름은 ?

       _____

       _____

       _____

    2. 미국인이 주로 거주하는곳에 사시는 것이 한국인이 주로 거주
       하는곳에 사는것 보다 더 마음이 편할 것 이라고 생각하십니까?

       (1) 분명히 그렇다 _____   (2) 아마 그럴 것이다. _____
       (3) 모르겠다 _____   (4) 아마 그렇지 않을 것이다._____
       (5) 분명히 그렇지 않다._____

    3. 미국사람을 한국사람보다 더 쉽게 친히 시귈 수 있다고
       생각하십니까?

       (1) 분명히 그렇다. _____   (2) 어느 정도 그렇다._____
       (3) 모르겠다. _____   (4) 어느 정도 그렇지 않다._____
       (5) 분명히 그렇지 않다._____

    4. 귀하의 개인문제를 마음털어 놓고 애기할 수 있는 미국인 친구가
       있읍니까?

       (1) 네명 또는 그 이상_____   (2) 세명_____(3) 두명 _____
       (4) 한명 _____(5) 한명도 없다. _____

116

5. 대부분의 미국인들의 귀하를 평등하게 받아드립니까?

(1) 전적으로 그렇다 _____ (2) 어느 정도 그렇다 _____
(3) 모르겠다 _____ (4) 어느 정도 그렇지않다. _____
(5) 전적으로 그렇지않다. _____

6. 환경이 허락한다면 자녀들이 미국 어린이들과 노는것이 한국인 어린이들만과 노는것 보다 좋다고 보십니까?

(1) 전적으로 그렇다 _____ (2) 어느정도 그렇다. _____
(3) 모르겠다. _____ (4) 어느정도 그렇지 않다. _____
(5) 전적으로 그렇지않다. _____

7. 한국인과 미국인 간의 결혼에 대해서 어떻게 생각하십니까?

(1) 전적으로 찬성 _____ (2) 어느정도 찬성 _____
(3) 모르겠다 _____ (4) 어느정도 불찬성 _____
(5) 전적으로 불찬성 _____

자유로운 의견 : _____
_____
_____
_____

8. 노후에 한국으로 돌아가셔서 여생을 지내시고 싶습니까?

(1) 전적으로 그렇다 _____ (2) 어느정도 그렇다. _____
(3) 모르겠다 _____ (4) 어느정도 그렇지않다. _____
(5) 전적으로 그렇지않다. _____

자유로운 의견 : _____
_____
_____

9. 지난 일년동안에 미국인 집으로 부터 초대를 받으신 적이 얼마나 됩니까? (주로 개인적인 친교를 위한 초대만)

대략 몇번 : _____

10. 지난 일년동안에 얼마나 자주 미국인 친지를 초대해서 대접 했읍니까? (주로 개인적인 친교를 위한 초대만)

대략 몇번 : _____

11. 귀하의 개인문제를 마음털어 놓고 얘기할 수 있는 한국인 친구가 있읍니까? (있다면 몇명이나?)

117

(1) 네명 또는 그 이상 _____ (2) 세명 _____
(3) 두명 _____ (4) 한명 _____
(5) 한명도 없다. _____

C. 기타 사항

1. 귀하의 미국인 동료들의 (같은 직장에서 같은 또는 비슷한 일을 하는) 수입에 비해서는 귀하의 수입이 대등하다고 보십니까?

(1) 전적으로 그렇다 _____ (2) 어느정도 그렇다 _____
(3) 모르겠다 _____ (4) 어느정도 그렇지 않다. _____
(5) 전적으로 그렇지 않다 _____

2. 귀하의 교육수준에 비해서 현 수입이 적합하다고 보십니까?

(1) 전적으로 그렇다 _____ (2) 어느정도 그렇다. _____
(3) 모르겠다 _____ (4) 어느정도 그렇지않다. _____
(5) 전적으로 그렇지않다. _____

3. 귀하의 교육수준에 비해서 현 직업이 적합하다고 보십니까?

(1) 전적으로 그렇다 _____ (2) 어느정도 그렇다 _____
(3) 모르겠다 _____ (4) 어느정도 그렇지않다 _____
(5) 전적으로 그렇지않다. _____

4. 일반적으로 보아 근면히 일하면 미국에서 성공할 기회가 있다고 보십니까? 만일 그렇다면 특히 어느면에서?

_____
_____
_____
_____

D. 인적사항 및 사회경제 배경

인적 사항

1. 성 별 _____ 2. 나이(만) _____

3. 결혼관계 (미혼, 기혼, 이혼, 기타) _____

4. 가족원 (동거자)

년 령	관 계	직 업(full-time, part-time

118

년 령	관 계	직 업(full-time, part-time

5. 미국 도착 일자(년, 월) _____

6. 시카고 도착일자 (년, 월)_____

7. 주택 (자기주택, 세집, 아파트, 기타)_____

사회 경제적 배경

1. 한국에서 받은 최종교육 (국민학교, 중고등, 대학, 대학원 학위 등) : _____

2. 한국을 떠날때 종사하던 직업 (상세한 직업적 활동 내용) : _____

3. 미국에서 받은 최종교육 (학위, 전공분야 등)

4. 현재직업(종사기관,직위, 직종등 상세한 활동 내용) _____

_____

5. 한국을 떠나기 직전 년 수입 (정기 년수입,부수입, 기타총액) _____

6. 미국 현재 년수입 (정기 년수입, 부수입, 기타총액) _____

E. 교회에 나가시는 경우 다음 사항에 대해서 대답해 주시면 감사 하겠읍니다.

1. 어느 교회에 나가시는지요 ? _____

119

2. 지난 일년 동안에 얼마나 자주 교회에 나가셨는지요 ?

(1) 매주 _____ (2) 한달에 두어번 _____
(3) 한달에 한번 _____ (4) 일년에 너덧 댓번 _____

3. 주일예배 (또는 미사)에 참석하시는 외에 다른 교회활동에도
참가 하십니까? 그렇다면 무슨 활동?

_____

4. 한국에 계실 때도 교회에 나가셨는지요 ? 그렇다면 얼마나
자주 ?

(1) 매주 _____ (2) 한달에 두어번 _____
(3) 한달에 한번 _____ (4) 일년에 너덧 댓번 _____

무슨 교회 _____

5. 현재 교회에 나가시므로서 어떤 면에서 만족감을 얻으시는지요?
불만한 점은 ?

_____
_____
_____
_____

6. 부모님의 종교는 ? _____

7. 조부모님의 종교는 ? _____

F. 귀하가 현재 당면하고 있는 애로, 곤란, 문제등이 무엇입니까?
(자유로운 대답) : _____

_____
_____
_____
_____

G. Interviewer's Observation and Comments:

120